Black Cat's Cooking Class Cookbook

To Marilyn —

Vanessa Daou
Antony Daou

Happy cooking & eating!

Tony 9/20/10

First published in 2009 in the United States
under the **BlackCat Imprint**,
a division of

Black Cat

Black Cat Ventures,
195 Main Street, Sharon Springs, NY 13459

ISBN # 978-0-9825666-9-5

Black Cat's Cooking Class Cookbook

a compilation of menus and recipes
from three years of cooking classes in Cooperstown

Black Cat Ventures LLC
195 Main Street
Sharon Springs
New York 13459

Black Cat

Visit the website ...

www.blackcat-ny.com

View products for sale ...

www.blackcat-alog.com

Foreword

The first version of this cookbook was intended for current and prospective cooking class participants and was limited to 400 copies. We were astonished that we sold them out at the Café in a little over three months --without any advertising or promotion at all.

We've gotten some wonderful compliments from readers and a few excellent suggestions. So we've decided to publish this second edition for a wider audience. It has some minor corrections and modifications, but is essentially the same cookbook.

We're also expanding the Café to add a second floor, which will include a demonstration kitchen for cooking classes. We've learned a lot from our class participants and readers and are very excited to be able to put together a space from the ground up with everything we've learned about successful, exciting and enlightening cooking classes. We're hoping to be done for the Christmas season.

So, as we look forward to another season of classes, we leave you with the hope that this book provides inspiration and a lot of happy cooking, and eating!

Tony Daou
Sharon Springs, October, 2009

Acknowledgements

This cookbook is dedicated with love to Veronica Gil Seaver (and to her late husband, Bob Seaver, whom we were privileged to know even for so short a time.) Veronica so graciously hosted these classes at her house at 160 Main Street in Cooperstown, and without her we'd have never done so many classes with so many wonderful people.

To all our wonderful "students" most especially Barbara Mulhern (who also proofread the drafts, and made excellent suggestions) and to Carla and Roger Macmillan, Rebecca and Henry Weil, Karin and David Svahn, Dottie and Hank Phillips, Katie and David Sanford, Maureen and Bob Moglia, Peg and John Leon, Sandy and Dick DeRosa, Cathy Raddatz, Kathy Chase, Cheryl and Peter Wright, Bruce and Kate Johnson, Amanda May, Neve Norton ... and all the rest, who taught us so much too!

Thank you to all our local suppliers including *Cooperstown Natural Foods*, *Ommegang Brewery*, *The Lemon Tree*, and especially to Chef Alex Webster of *Alex and Ika* restaurant in Cooperstown, who was always there for us when we ran out of something at the last minute. A special thank you to Ulla Adema, Vanessa's mother.

And, finally, we thank our children, Sebastian, Nicholas, Isabella, Adrian and Julian, who put up with our absences, tasted everything, and whom we adore.

Tony and Vanessa Daou
Sharon Springs, April 2009

Index of Classes and Recipes

Introduction

We started giving cooking classes in 2005 when we opened the Black Cat Café and Bakery in the tiny historic spa village of Sharon Springs, NY. There is not much to do in upstate NY in the long winters, and the classes took off. In winter 2006, our dear friend Veronica Seaver suggested we do a few in her house in Cooperstown, so that more people from there could join in. What began as a couple of classes here and there soon turned into two or three a week between January and March. The classes are small, usually 8-12 people, never more than 20 or so. And while we still do some cooking classes at the Café, the group of people and the venue have become a major part of our past 3 winters (and hopefully many more to come.)

Vanessa typically does most of the day classes on her own. They are usually smaller and are about 2 hours long, and focus on recipes, either baking or one-pot and lunch recipes.

On the other hand, the dinner classes are usually about 3 ½ hours long, with both Vanessa and Tony (although our eldest son Sebastian, a freshman at RPI, has filled in for Tony a couple of times.) These classes are based on our belief that you can prepare a fabulous, interesting dinner to entertain friends (or make it with them) in about 2 -2 ½ hours. So we start at 6PM with the longest recipe and pace ourselves. About 45 minutes or so into the class, we prepare and taste one of the appetizers, with a glass of wine. By 8:30 we all sit down to dinner. We discuss the recipes, our thoughts and requests and plans for the next classes.

So here is the collection of the recipes from those classes. The lunch and dinner classes are focused around complete meals that you can prepare at home, and we think make excellent menus for entertaining. Please join us.

Day Classes - Lunch

One-pot Meal Inspired by Jacques, 2/3/09

- **Roast Veal with Artichokes**
- **A New One-pot Bread**
- **Cucumber and Watercress Salad**
- **Broiled Grapefruit with Meringue**

Jacques Pépin has always been one of our favorite sources for good cooking, masterful in his technique, yet always with a home-spun touch. We fell in love with his style from his TV show in the 90's. The bread is adapted from one he made on a recent WKQED show. The broiled grapefruit recipe is an old favorite from Vanessa's mother, Ulla.

.

Roast Veal with Artichokes

- 3 lb boneless veal roast
- salt and black pepper
- 3 tsp fresh thyme leaves
- 2 tbsp unsalted butter
- 2 tbsp virgin olive oil
- 6 fresh artichokes
- 12 medium onions, peeled
- 12 large cloves garlic, peeled
- 2 tomatoes, seeded, and cut into half-inch pieces
- 2 tbsp soy sauce

Preheat oven to 400°F. Tie the roast with twine if necessary, and sprinkle with about ½ tsp each of salt and pepper and the thyme. In an oven proof skillet, heat the butter and oil. When hot, add the meat, and brown it on all sides for a total of about 8-10 minutes. Remove the roast to a platter, and reserve the drippings in the skillet.

Cut off the top third of the artichokes and trim off the thorny projections on the remaining leaves. Cut the trimmed artichokes in quarters. Remove and discard the chokes. Add the cut artichokes, onions, garlic, and remaining salt and pepper to the drippings in the skillet, and toss the vegetables to coat them thoroughly.

Arrange the roast on top of the vegetables, and place the pan in a 400°F oven for 20 minutes. Turn the roast over, stirring the vegetables, and return the pan to the oven for another 20 minutes.

Stir in the tomatoes, soy sauce, and 2-3 tbsp water, and cook for 10 more minutes, for a total cooking time of 1 hour, not including the browning.

Remove the roast from the oven, and allow to rest for 10-15 minutes before carving. Serve surrounded with artichokes and onions.

Serves 6.

Cucumber and Watercress Salad

- 2 large English cucumbers, peeled, halved and seeded
- 1 bunch fresh watercress
- ½ cup Kalamata olives, chopped
- 1 red onion, quartered and sliced thinly
- 1 red, yellow or orange bell pepper cut in ½" pieces
- 6 plum tomatoes, cored and diced
- 6 oz crumbled feta cheese

Black Olive Vinaigrette

- ¼ cup red wine vinegar
- 1 ½ cup Kalamata olives
- 3 garlic cloves, peeled
- 6 tbsp capers
- 1 lemon, juiced
- 1 cup olive oil

Purée ingredients for vinaigrette until smooth in a food processor. Set aside. Mix salad ingredients together, then just before serving, mix well with the vinaigrette, and garnish with feta. Serves 8.

No-knead, All-in-one-pot Bread

- 2½ cups lukewarm water
- 2 tsp salt
- 1 tsp yeast
- 4 cups flour

This new version of no-knead bread is from Jacques Pépin. We like the fact that it is all in a single pot, but it doesn't produce the same quality of bread in our opinion.

Combine all the ingredients in a non-stick pot. Stir with a spatula for about a minute or until a gooey dough forms. Cover with lid, and proof at room temp for 60-90 minutes.

Stir the dough with spatula to break the first rise. Replace the lid, and refrigerate overnight or for about 12 hours.

Bake uncovered in a preheated oven at 425°F. After 40-45 minutes cover loosely with aluminum foil if it is starting to brown. Cook for about 15 minutes more. Let cool and deflate about 5 minutes before removing from the pot.

Broiled Grapefruits with Meringue

- 2 grapefruits, halved crosswise
- 2 large egg whites
- 1/8 tsp salt
- 1/2 cup packed sugar

Preheat broiler, with rack in middle position. Put the egg whites and salt in the bowl of an electric mixer fitted with a whisk attachment, and beat on medium speed until frothy, about 30 seconds. Raise speed to high, and add sugar 1 tbsp at a time, beating until incorporated. Continue to beat until the egg whites hold stiff peaks (like marshmallow fluff).

Place grapefruit halves on a large plate and carefully cut between membranes to loosen segments completely. Place meringue in a large pastry bag, snip off the end with a scissors and pipe one-quarter of meringue onto each half. Transfer to a baking pan. Broil, checking frequently, until meringues start to brown, about 5 minutes. Move rack to bottom position of oven and cook about 5 minutes more, making sure meringue doesn't burn. Serve immediately.

Serves 4.

Bread and Soups, 1/30/08

- **Pork Noodle Soup with Cinnamon and Star Anise**
- **Lebanese Bean Soup, *Makhloutah***
- **Wild Rice and Tomato Soup**

- **No-Knead Bread** (see page 76.)

This class featured a repeat of the one-pot bread, plus three great soups, in three different traditions – from the Far East, the Mediterranean and the Middle East.

Pork Noodle Soup with Cinnamon and Star Anise

- 3 lb country-style pork ribs
- 6 cups water
- 1 cup soy sauce
- 1 cup rice wine or a dry sherry
- ¼ cup packed dark brown sugar
- 1 head garlic, halved crosswise
- 3-4 cinnamon sticks
- 1 whole star anise
- 6 ounces bean thread (cellophane) noodles
- chopped cilantro and scallions for garnish

Cut from the blade end of the pork loin, next to the shoulder, country-style ribs contain a lot of fat (and hence flavor), and may or may not contain bone. Gently simmer all ingredients except noodles in a 6-quart heavy pot, covered, skimming as needed, until pork is very tender, 1½ to 2 hours.

Transfer pork to a bowl. Discard bones, spices, and garlic. Coarsely shred meat. Skim fat from broth, then return meat and bring to a simmer. Rinse noodles, then stir into broth and simmer, uncovered, stirring occasionally, until noodles are translucent and tender, about 6 minutes. Garnish with cilantro and scallions.

Serves 6.

Wild Rice and Tomato Soup

- 5 tbsp olive oil
- 1 large onion, diced
- 2 carrots, diced
- 2 stalks celery, diced
- 4 cups crushed tomatoes
- ½ cup wild rice
- 4 or more cups vegetable broth or chicken stock
- 2 tsp salt
- 2 tsp black pepper
- 2 tbsp fresh or dried basil
- 4 sprigs of parsley for garnish

One of the all-time favorites at the Café, this soup is great year-round.

Heat oil in large pot.

Add onion, carrot and celery. Cook until vegetables are translucent, stirring.

Drain tomatoes, then pour into pot with the stock and rice. Bring to boil, cover, and reduce heat to a simmer. Add salt, pepper, sugar, and herbs. Stir often, and cook until rice starts to split, about 1 ½ hours.

Garnish with parsley.

Serves 4.

Lebanese Bean Soup, *Makhloutah*

- 1/3 cup cannellini beans
- ½ cup whole dried chickpeas
- ½ tsp baking soda
- ¾ cup brown lentils
- 11 cups water
- 1/8 cup coarse bulgar wheat
- 1/8 cup white short-grain rice

- ½ cup + 2 tbsp olive oil
- 2 onions, finely chopped
- 1 tsp ground cinnamon
- 1 tsp ground cumin
- 2 tsp ground allspice
- black pepper and salt to taste

The night before, put the beans and chickpeas to soak in 3 times their volume of water, and stir in the baking soda.

Wash the bulgar, rice and lentils separately in several changes of cold water, drain and set aside. Put the lentils in a large saucepan. Rinse the beans and chickpeas under cold water, drain, and add to lentils. Pour in the water, cover the pan and place over high heat. Bring to a boil, then reduce heat to medium and boil gently, covered for an hour, or until tender.

Fry the chopped onion in the oil over medium heat until golden. Add the onions along with the rice and bulgar to the legumes when they are tender. Season with the spices, and simmer for 15 minutes. Adjust seasoning and thickness to taste.

Serves 4-6.

Indian Luncheon, 1/17/08

- Quick Pan Bread, *Chapati*
- Chick Pea Special, *Khatte Chole*
- Lamb with Peas and Yoghurt, *Keema Matar*
- Puree of Lentils, *Dal*

A note about the penchant for aged Basmati Rice.
Basmati is long grain rice, famous for its fragrance and delicate flavor. The grains are much longer than they are wide. They actually grow longer as they cook, and stay firm and separate cooked. Does it matter if it is aged? Not really. And if you cannot find Basmati, jasmine rice is just as good for these recipes.

Quick Pan Bread, *Chapati*, see recipe page 56.

Chickpea Special, *Khatte Chole*

A favorite *chole* recipe comes from Madhur Jaffrey, the renowned Indian writer. It recreates some of the roadside vendor flavor of this Indian "fast food."

- 12 oz chickpeas soaked overnight or 1 12 oz can cooked chickpeas
- 4 pints water
- 1 medium onion, finely chopped
- 2 tsp salt
- 1 fresh green chili, chopped
- 1 tbsp ginger, grated
- 4 tbsp lemon juice
- 6 tbsp oil
- 1 tomato, chopped
- 1 tbsp ground coriander
- 1 tbsp ground cumin
- ½ tsp turmeric
- 2 tsp garam masala
- ½ tsp cayenne pepper

Mix about 2 tbsp of the chopped onion with ginger, green chili, lemon juice and a pinch of salt and set aside (it'll turn a pretty pink.) Cook chickpeas in the water in a large pot till tender. Then add ½ tsp each of cumin, coriander and turmeric and salt.

Heat the oil in a heavy pot, add remaining onion, and fry till you see reddish spots, about 8-10 minutes. Add tomato and sauté for another 5 minutes, mashing tomato further with a slotted spoon. Add remaining coriander, cumin and turmeric. Stir for 30 seconds; add drained chickpeas, salt to taste, garam masala and cayenne. Cook for 8-10 more minutes, stirring occasionally.

Serves 4.

Red Lentil Puree, *Dal*

- 1 ½ cups red lentils
- 2 garlic cloves, peeled and finely chopped
- 2" piece sliced peeled fresh ginger
- 1 tsp chopped coriander
- 1 tsp ground turmeric
- 5 cups water
- ¼ tsp cayenne pepper
- 2 tsp salt
- 2 tbsp lemon juice
- 2 tbsp vegetable oil or ghee
- 1 pinch asafoetida powder
- 1 tsp whole cumin seeds
- 6 lime wedges for garnish

Clean and wash the lentils thoroughly. Put them in heavy-bottomed 4 quart pot, add water, and bring to a boil. Remove the froth and scum that collects on the top. Now add the garlic, ginger, turmeric, and cayenne. Cover, leaving the lid very slightly ajar. Lower heat to simmer gently for about 1½ hours.

Stir occasionally. When the dal is cooked, add the salt and lemon juice (it should be thicker than pea soup, but thinner than cooked cereal.) In a small skillet or pot, heat the vegetable oil or ghee over a medium-high flame. When hot, add the asafoetida and cumin seeds. As soon as the asafoetida sizzles and expands and the cumin seeds turn dark (this will take only a few seconds), pour the oil and spices over lentils and serve.

Garnish with chopped coriander, and serve with lime wedges on the edge of the bowl.

You can serve with plain rice and a vegetable for a simple meal. Most meat and chicken dishes go well with this dal.

Serves 6.

Keema Matar

- 1 cup plain yoghurt
- ½ tsp ground turmeric
- ¼ tsp cayenne pepper
- 1 tsp ground cumin
- 1 tbsp ground coriander
- 1-2 tsp salt
- 3" pc of finely grated peeled fresh ginger
- 4 garlic cloves peeled and crushed
- 2 lbs ground lamb or lean beef
- 3 sticks cinnamon
- 4 whole cardamom pods
- 3 bay leaves
- ½ cup pureed tomatoes
- 2 cups shelled peas
- 1-2 fresh hot green chili peppers, finely chopped
- 1 ½ tsp garam masala
- 2 tbsp chopped fresh cilantro leaves
- vegetable oil for cooking

Put the yoghurt in a bowl and whisk lightly until smooth and creamy. Add turmeric, cayenne, cumin, coriander, salt, ginger and garlic. Mix until well blended. Put the meat into a large bowl. Pour yoghurt mixture over the top and mix with hands until thoroughly blended. Generously coat a large non-stick sauté pan with the cooking oil and set over medium-high heat. When hot, add cinnamon, cardamom and bay leaves and stir a couple of times. Stir in the onion and fry about 5 minutes or until the onion pieces are reddish brown

Add the meat, and stir breaking meat apart until no lumps or pinkness is left, about 5 minutes. Stir in the tomato puree. Bring to a simmer and cover. Cook 30 minutes on medium-low heat stirring every 6-7 minutes to make sure there is enough liquid and meat doesn't stick to bottom. Once most of the liquid has gone, remove the cover. Take out the cinnamon sticks, bay leaves and cardamom pods, and fry for another 5 minutes uncovered.

Spoon out as much of the fat as you can, then add the peas, green chili, fresh coriander (cilantro), the garam masala and about 6 tablespoons water. Cover, lower heat and simmer another 6-7 minutes or until peas are cooked.

Serves 4-6 with rice.

Three One-Pot Meals, 2/27/08

- Chicken Pot Pie with Biscuit Crust
- Lebanese Spinach and Lentil Soup
- Belgian Beef Carbonnade

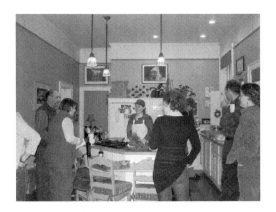

Chicken Pot Pie with Biscuit Crust

Filling:
- 4 cups chicken broth
- 4 carrots, diced
- 2 lb red potatoes, diced
- 3 celery stalks, diced
- 3 cups cooked chicken, cubed
- 1 onion, chopped
- 6 tbsp unsalted butter
- 6 tbsp flour
- ½ tsp thyme
- ¼ tsp nutmeg
- ½ cup minced fresh parsley
- salt and pepper to taste

Biscuit Crust:
- 1 1/3 cups flour
- 1 1/2 tsp baking powder
- 1/2 tsp baking soda
- ¾ tsp salt
- 2 tbsp butter, cut into bits
- 2 tbsp shortening, cut into bits
- 1/2 cup Cheddar cheese, grated
- 1 large egg
- 1/3 cup buttermilk

Egg Wash:
- 1 egg yolk
- 2 tbsp milk

In a saucepan bring broth to a boil, and add carrots, potatoes, and celery. Simmer until vegetables are tender, about 10-12 minutes. Transfer them to a bowl, reserving the broth, and add the chicken to the bowl.

In another saucepan, cook the onion in the butter over medium-low heat, stirring, until it is softened. Add flour and cook, stirring, for 3 minutes. Add 3 cups of broth in a stream, whisking. Bring mixture to a boil, whisking. Add the thyme and simmer the sauce, stirring occasionally, for 5 minutes. Stir in nutmeg, parsley, and salt and pepper to taste. Pour sauce over the chicken and vegetables. Mix gently, until it is just combined. Transfer mixture to a 2-qt. baking dish.

In a bowl, sift together the flour, baking powder, baking soda, and salt. Add the butter and shortening and blend the mixture until it resembles cornmeal. Add the cheese and toss together.

Break egg into a measuring cup and add buttermilk to it so that the total volume is ½ cup. Beat with a fork. Add to the flour mixture, stirring until the mixture just forms a dough. Gather the dough into a ball and, on a floured surface, pat it out ½" thick. Cut as many rounds as possible using a 2-inch biscuit cutter, dipped in flour. Gather the scraps and pat and cut again.

Arrange the rounds on the chicken mixture. Beat the egg yolk with the milk and brush the tops of the biscuits with the wash. Prick biscuits with a fork.

Bake in the middle of a preheated 450° oven for 20-25 minutes, or until the biscuits are puffed and golden, and the filling is bubbling.

Serves 6.

Belgian Beef Carbonnade

- 2 tbsp butter
- 6 onions thinly sliced
- 2 ½ lb pounds boneless beef cut in 2" pieces
- 3 tbsp flour
- salt and pepper
- 1 pint rich Belgian ale, like **Ommegang Hennepin**
- 1 tbsp brown sugar
- 1 tbsp vinegar
- 6-8 slices French bread
- Dijon mustard to taste

Brown the onions in the butter in a Dutch oven. Shake the beef pieces in flour.

Remove the onions and set aside. Brown the beef pieces in batches. When done return all the beef and the onions to the pot.

Add the beer and bring to a boil. Add the sugar, salt and pepper. Cover, and bake in a 375°F oven for about 2 hours.

Spread the French bread with Dijon to taste. About 45 minutes before the end, uncover, and add the vinegar and bread slices on top. Bake uncovered for the last 45 minutes.

Serves 8.

Lebanese Spinach and Lentil Soup, *Addas b'Sbanegh*

- 1 cup brown lentils, rinsed and drained
- 8 cups water
- salt to taste
- ½ cup finely chopped cilantro
- 2 large onions, finely chopped
- 5 cloves garlic, crushed
- ½ lb. spinach leaves or Swiss chard, washed and chopped
- 1 cup finely chopped flat-leaf parsley
- ½ cup lemon juice
- Vegetable or olive oil for cooking (don't use extra-virgin)

Place the lentils, water and salt in a pot and cook over medium heat until the lentils are tender, but still intact and even slightly firm.

In the meantime, coat a non-stick skillet with a generous coating of olive oil and place over medium heat. Fry the onions and garlic together in the oil, stirring frequently, then add the cilantro and cook until the onions are golden brown.

Add the fried mixture with its oil to the lentils, and then stir in the spinach, parsley and lemon juice.

Simmer until spinach is cooked through. Serve immediately.

Serves 6.

Two One-Pot Meals and a New Bread, 1/30/09

- **Quick Hanoi Beef Noodle Soup**
- **Galician Garbanzo soup**
- **Tibetan Flatbread**

This class featured a quick version of *Pho Bo*. The traditional version of this Vietnamese specialty has to be started at least a day in advance, and calls for a beef stock made from scratch, including charring onions and ginger first. This version takes just 30 minutes and serves 4 for a wonderful one-pot meal.

Galician Garbanzo Soup is inspired by Mollie Katzen's Moosewood Cookbook, and is a much-imitated mainstay of vegetarian cooking.

For this quick bread, we are again indebted to Jacques Pepin, who says that the dough is actually similar to Irish soda bread, but he cooks it in a non-stick skillet.

Quick Hanoi Beef Noodle Soup, *Pho Bo*

- 6 cups beef broth
- 1 slice ginger, 1/2" thick
- 2 whole star anise
- 1 cinnamon stick
- ½ lb. piece boneless sirloin, trimmed of fat and frozen
- 3 ounces dried flat rice noodles (pad thai)
- 1/3 cup Asian fish sauce (nuoc mam)
- salt and black pepper
- 1 cup fresh bean sprouts, rinsed and drained
- ¼ cup minced scallions
- ¼ cup chopped cilantro,
- 1 small thin fresh Asian chili, sliced very thin
- ½ cup fresh basil leaves (thin-leaved Asian basil if you can find it)
- lime wedges for garnish

In a 2 quart saucepan bring broth, ginger, star anise, and cinnamon to a boil. Reduce heat and simmer for 15 minutes. In a large bowl soak noodles in hot water to cover 15 minutes, or until softened and pliable. While noodles are soaking, bring a kettle of salted water to a boil for noodles. Drain noodles in a colander and cook in boiling water, stirring 45 seconds, or until tender. Drain noodles in a colander again and set aside.

Strain broth into saucepan and bring to a boil. Stir in fish sauce, salt and pepper. With a very sharp knife cut the frozen piece of sirloin across the grain into paper-thin slices. Add the sirloin strips and the sprouts and cook just 30-45 seconds, or until sirloin changes color. Skim any froth from soup. To serve, divide noodles into 4 bowls. Ladle soup over noodles. Sprinkle scallion greens, cilantro, chilies and basil over soup and serve with lime wedges

Serves 6.

Galician Garbanzo Soup

- 3 cups cooked or 3 (15-oz) cans garbanzo beans (chickpeas)
- 5 cups vegetable broth
- 1 tbsp olive oil
- 1 ½ cups chopped onion
- 2 tbsp crushed garlic
- 1 potato, diced
- 2 carrots, diced
- 2 celery stalks, diced
- 1 bay leaf
- 1 tsp dry mustard
- 1 tsp ground cumin
- ¼ tsp saffron
- 1 cup green peas
- 1 tbsp red wine vinegar
- 1 ripe medium-size tomato, peeled, seeded, chopped
- salt, black pepper and cayenne pepper to taste
- minced fresh basil

Rinse and thoroughly drain the garbanzo beans. Place about ⅔ of them in a blender or food processor with 2 cups of the stock and purée until mostly smooth. Set aside. Place a soup pot over medium heat and add olive oil and swirl to coat the pan. Sauté onion 6-8 minutes or until onion is translucent.

Add half the garlic plus the potato, carrot, celery and salt, and sauté for another 5 minutes or so. Add the garbanzo purée, plus remaining stock and garbanzo beans, and the bay leaf, mustard, cumin, and saffron. Bring to boil, then lower heat, cover and simmer for about 30 minutes, stirring occasionally. Stir in the remaining garlic, plus the peas, vinegar, and tomato.

Taste to correct salt, and then add black pepper and cayenne to taste. Simmer for about 5 minutes longer.

Serves 8.

Tibetan Flatbread

- 1 ½ cups all-purpose flour
- 1 tsp baking powder
- 1 tsp salt
- 1 cup water, plus 3 tbsp more for steaming the bread
- 1 tbsp olive oil

Combine the flour, baking powder, and salt in a medium bowl. Add the cup of water and mix together with a sturdy rubber spatula to create a thick gooey dough.

Spread the oil in a cold 12-inch nonstick skillet with a cover. Add the dough to the skillet. Dip the spatula into the oil (to prevent the dough from sticking to it) in the skillet and use it to press on the dough to flatten it in the skillet.

Add the remaining water to create a bit of steam and get the bread cooking. Cover and place over medium-high heat for about 10 minutes. The water should be gone and the dough should be frying at this point. Reduce the heat and, using a fork, turn the bread over. Cover and cook for another 5 minutes. Uncover and set aside to cool in the skillet. Remove, cut into wedges and serve.

Serves 4.

One-pot Meals from Around the World, 2/17/09

- *Loubia b'Zeit*, **Lebanese Green Beans**
- **Risotto Verde**
- **Chickpea and Carrot Salad**
- **Honey Madeleines**

Loubia b'Zeit, or Green Beans in Olive Oil, is a classic Lebanese dish of green beans in tomato sauce.

Risotto Verde is interesting for 2 reasons -- this Spring-inspired vegetarian version of the classic Italian dish combines asparagus and spinach, and has much less cheese -- it is also baked in the oven. Unlike the intensive classic version, the preparation time is less than 10 minutes.

The other 2 recipes, both inspired by *Once Upon A Tart*, rounded out our luncheon that day.

Chickpea and Carrot Salad

- 2 cups cooked or 2 15-oz cans chickpeas
- 1 cup black olives, pitted
- 4 carrots, coarsely grated
- ½ cup chopped cilantro
- 4 scallions, halved lengthwise and sliced very thin
- 2 cloves garlic, peeled and minced
- zest and juice of 1 lemon
- 2 tbsp ground cumin
- 2 tsp paprika
- ¼ tsp cayenne pepper
- salt and black pepper
- ¼ cup extra-virgin olive oil

Drain and rinse chickpeas, and put in a large bowl. Chop the olives coarsely, and then add to the chick peas. Add carrots, cilantro and scallions. Make the vinaigrette by whisking the remaining ingredients except the olive oil together. Then add the oil in a small steady stream, whisking as you go to form an emulsion. Pour over salad and toss well. Chill for at least an hour before serving. Serves 4.

Lebanese Green Bean Casserole, *Loubia b'Zeit*

- 1 ½ lb fresh green beans
- 1 ½ lb ripe tomatoes, peeled and chopped
- 1 large onion, finely chopped
- 8 unpeeled cloves of garlic
- 6 tbsp olive oil
- salt to taste

Top, tail and de-string the green beans, and chop them into 2-3" pieces. Heat the olive oil in a pan over a medium heat. Add the chopped onions and garlic and sauté until they turn golden, about 10 minutes. Add the beans, sprinkle with a generous pinch of salt and sauté for a few minutes, or till the beans turn glossy and bright green. Pour in the tomatoes, add salt to taste, mix well and cover the pan. Boil gently for about 40 minutes or until the sauce has thickened and the beans are done to your liking. Serve warm (it is also delicious cold) with warmed pita bread. Serves 4-6 with rice.

Quick Risotto with Spinach and Asparagus, *Risotto Verde*

- 4 cups loosely packed fresh spinach
- 12 asparagus spears
- 1 tbsp extra-virgin olive oil
- ¾ cup minced onion
- salt and white pepper to taste
- 1 cup Arborio rice
- 2 cups vegetable or chicken stock
- 1/4 tsp freshly grated nutmeg
- ¾ cup freshly grated Parmesan cheese

Preheat oven to 400 °F.

Wash, rinse, dry and chop the spinach. Trim the woody ends off the asparagus, and then cut into 1-2 inch pieces.

Combine oil, onion and salt in large saucepan over medium heat. Stir and cook until onion is soft, about 4 minutes. Add the rice, and stir to coat with oil. Add stock, spinach, asparagus, nutmeg and additional salt, if desired. Bring just to a simmer. Stir in half the cheese.

Transfer mixture to a 1.5-quart baking dish and smooth the top. Sprinkle remaining cheese over, then cover dish. Bake for until rice is cooked through and has absorbed the liquid, about 35-40 minutes.

Rice should be moist. Serve at once.

Serves 6-8.

Honey Madeleines

- 4 tbsp unsalted butter, plus more, melted, for brushing the pans
- 1 tbsp honey
- 1 tsp vanilla extract
- 2 large eggs
- 4 tsp dark brown sugar
- ¾ cup all-purpose flour
- 1 tsp baking powder
- ½ tsp salt
- confectioner's sugar for dusting

Melt butter, stir in honey and vanilla extract, and let cool to room temperature. Beat eggs and sugars together in a big bowl, until eggs are foamy and light in color. In a separate small bowl, whisk flour, baking powder and salt. Then fold the dry ingredients into the wet, stopping as soon as no flour is visible.

Pour in the butter/honey mixture, and continue mixing until all ingredients are combined. Preheat oven to 425°, and place a rack in the center. Brush your Madeleine molds with melted butter. Now, take a spoonful of batter, and pushing it off with your finger, or piping through a plastic bag, and fill each mold to ¾ full.

Place mold on the center rack and bake 8-10 minutes or until they are puffed up above the edge of the mold and each has a bump on it. Don't over-bake – be sure to remove when edges are golden-brown. Dust with powdered sugar.

Makes 12 madeleines.

Brunch Specials, 3/17/08

- **German Apple Pancake**
- ***Poffertjes*, Dutch mini-Crumpets**
- **Butter-crumbed Eggs**
- ***Torta Milanese***

Butter-crumbed eggs are a wonderful recipe inspired by Marion Cunningham. We serve it at the cafe on special occasions. They are sort of like Scotch Eggs, but we think better. The combination of crunch and silky softness is divine.

Poffertjes, to be made properly really require a special pan, but are fairly easy to make.

The apple pancake and the Torta Milanese take much less effort than you'd imagine, and each is a real treat.

Butter-crumbed Eggs

- 4 poached eggs
- 2 raw eggs lightly beaten
- 1 stick of butter

- 2 cups fresh bread crumbs mixed with salt and pepper to taste

Poach eggs and blot them dry. Melt butter in a large skillet over medium heat. Now, while the butter is melting, dip the poached eggs first in the raw egg then in the crumbs to coat well.

When the butter has melted, gently place the breaded eggs into the skillet and fry until golden on both sides, flipping once. Remove from skillet, and serve immediately.

Dutch Crumpets, *Poffertjes*

- 1 lb 2 oz self-rising flour
- 2 large eggs
- 1 lb 12 oz milk

- 1 tsp vanilla extract
- a pinch of salt
- oil for brushing the pan

Sift flour in a large bowl. Combine milk, eggs and vanilla extract in a bowl and mix lightly. Add the wet mixture to the flour and beat well for 3-5 minutes till the batter is light and fluffy. Cover and stand batter for an hour. Pour batter into a squeeze bottle.

Place the Poffertje pan on the stovetop at medium heat. Spray pan with oil. When the oil is hot, squeeze the batter into each hole, filling it just below the rim. When bubbles start appearing in the batter, flip over each pancake gently in their holes with a butter knife. Cook the other side for 2-3 minutes and slide the pancakes onto a plate.

Torta Milanese

- 8 large eggs
- 4 oz water
- 4 tbsp chopped tarragon
- 2 lbs spinach, blanched and chopped
- 1 large onion chopped
- 2 tbsp olive oil
- 8 oz grated Gruyère cheese
- 2 sheets puff pastry, thawed cut into two 9" circles and one 9x3" strip
- salt and pepper to taste
- 1 egg mixed with 1 tbsp water for egg wash

Preheat oven to 350°F. In a large skillet, heat oil and sauté the onion. After blanching spinach, be sure to squeeze out all the water and chop coarsely. Combine spinach with the sautéed onion, and remove from heat. Add salt and pepper to taste.

Whisk eggs well with water and tarragon. Heat a large non-stick pan, grease well and cook a third of the egg mixture. When set, remove from pan and make 2 more omelets the same way.

Grease a 10" spring form pan. Place one of puff pastry circles in the bottom of a spring form pan and strip of puff pastry around the edge of the pan. Top with 1 omelet, then half the spinach mixture and half of the cheese. Follow this with the second omelet, the second half of the spinach mixture and the remainder of the cheese.

Top this all with the last omelet and the second puff pastry circle. Fold down the edges of the puff pastry. Cut slits in the top, brush with egg wash and bake 35-40 minutes, until golden brown.   Serve warm.

Serves 6-8.

German Apple Pancake

- 3 large eggs
- ¾ cup milk
- ¾ cup white flour
- ½ tsp salt
- 2 tbsp unsalted butter
- ¾ cup thinly-sliced apples

For the filling:
- 1 lb tart apples, sliced
- 4 tbsp unsalted butter
- ¼ cup sugar
- 1 tsp cinnamon
- powdered sugar for dusting

Preheat oven to 450° F. Beat together eggs, milk, flour and salt until very smooth. Add some the sliced apples.

In a heavy 12" skillet, melt the butter. As soon as it is quite hot, pour in the batter, and put the skillet in the oven. After about 15 minutes, lower oven temperature to 350°F and bake for another 10 minutes, or until the pancake is light brown and crisp. Keep an eye on it for the first 10 or 15 minutes of baking, the pancake may puff up in large bubbles. If it does, pierce thoroughly with a knife or fork.

While pancake is baking, prepare the apple filling. Peel and thinly slice a pound of tart apples. Heat 4 tbsp of butter in a skillet and add the apples, sugar and cinnamon. The apples should be cooked for 8-10 minutes over a medium flame until just tender, and not soft. (The filling can be prepared ahead of time and reheated for serving.)

Once the pancake is ready, slide it onto an oval platter and pour the hot filling on one side. Drizzle with a little melted butter, then fold the other side over. Dust with powdered sugar and serve immediately.

Serves 6-8.

An Asian Sampler, 3/3/08

- **Quick Pork Dumplings**
- **Vietnamese-style Spring Rolls**
- **Peking-style Duck in Pancakes**

Quick Pork Dumplings

- 24 wonton wrappers
- 3" piece of fresh ginger, peeled and finely chopped
- 10 tbsp soy sauce
- 1 bunch scallions
- 1 lb ground pork (from shoulder; not lean)

Combine half the soy sauce with ginger in a small bowl. Finely chop the scallions (reserving about 2 tsp scallions for garnish) and put them in a bowl along with the pork, finely chopped ginger, and the remaining soy sauce. Gently knead the pork with your hands until just combined. Chill, covered, for 10 minutes.

To form dumplings: Line a large baking sheet with paper towels and dust lightly with flour. Put a wonton wrapper on the fingers of one hand near the palm and put 2 slightly rounded teaspoons of the pork mixture in the center of a round. Fold dough in half, enclosing filling, and pinch edges together to seal. Put finished dumpling on lined baking sheet and form more dumplings in same manner. Cover loosely with paper towels.

Gently drop the dumplings into a 6 quart pot of boiling water, gently stirring once to prevent sticking, and cook about 6 minutes. Dumplings will float to top while cooking. Transfer dumplings with a slotted spoon to a serving dish and sprinkle with reserved scallions.

Ginger Dipping Sauce, mix together:

- ¼ cup rice-wine vinegar
- ¼ cup light soy sauce
- 2 tbsp sugar
- 1 tbsp sesame oil
- 2 scallions, thinly sliced
- 2 tsp grated peeled ginger

47

Vietnamese-style Spring Rolls

- 3 tsp olive oil
- 3 tsp minced fresh ginger
- 20 uncooked medium shrimp, peeled, de-veined, halved lengthwise
- ½   cup chopped cilantro
- 4 cups hot water
- salt and pepper to taste
- 10 rice-paper sheets
- 5 small lettuce leaves, halved
- 2/3 cup thin strips green onions
- 2/3 cup thin strips seeded cucumber
- 5 tsp minced fresh mint

Heat oil in a medium skillet over medium-high heat. Add ginger and sauté until fragrant, about 20 seconds. Add shrimp and cilantro; sauté until shrimp are just cooked through, about 1 minute . Remove from heat. Season with salt and pepper.

Pour hot water into large bowl. Using tongs, dip 1 rice paper spring-roll sheet in water 5 seconds. Remove and place on wet towel. Let stand 30 seconds (spring-roll sheet should be soft and pliable; if still stiff, sprinkle with a little hot water).

Place half of lettuce leaf across top third of spring-roll sheet. Arrange 4 shrimp halves on lettuce. Top with about 1 tbsp each of green onions and cucumber. Sprinkle ½ tsp mint over filling. Fold sides of spring-roll sheet over ends of filling. Starting at filled side, roll into cylinder. Place on plate. Repeat with remaining spring-roll sheets, lettuce, shrimp, green onions, cucumber and mint. Slice in half diagonally. Makes 10.

Nam Pla **Dipping Sauce:** Mix in together:

- 1/3 cup fish sauce (*nam pla*)
- 3 tbsp thinly sliced scallions
- 2 tbsp fresh lime juice
- pinch of dried red pepper

Peking-style Duck in Pancakes

- roasted duck, whole (or breasts only) warmed, meat sliced in thin strips
- 4 scallions, sliced in rounds
- hoisin sauce
- 2 cucumbers, in thin 3" sticks

Pancakes

- 2½ cups flour
- ½ tsp salt
- 1 cup boiling water
- vegetable oil for brushing

Combine flour and salt. Gradually add water, blending with a fork until the mixture is the size of peas. Divide dough in half. Form one half into a ball, keeping the rest covered to prevent drying out. Knead until the dough is soft and smooth, about 5 min. Shape into a roll about 18" long. Cut into 16 pieces. Cover with a damp cloth.

Place two pieces on a lightly floured surface. Pat each into a three inch circle. Generously brush the tops with oil. Place one on top of the other with the oiled sides touching. Flour a rolling pin and roll the rounds out to 8" circles. Turn frequently to insure even rolling. Heat an un-greased skillet over medium heat. Cook the pancake two to three minutes until browned, then turn and repeat for the second side.

Remove from pan and quickly separate the two pancakes. Stack them, browned side up, and cover with foil. Repeat to make 16 pancakes.

To assemble, brush center of pancake with hoisin sauce. Make a line of duck strips, then cucumber slices and scallions. Fold up about 1 ½" of the bottom, then roll into a cylinder. You can prepare in advance, or better yet, allow guest to prepare to their taste.

Bread and Soup, inspired by Staff Meals from Chanterelle, 3/3/09

- **No-knead Bread (Repeat)**
- **Hot Beef Borscht**
- **Mushroom-barley Soup**
- **Spiced-up Honey Cake**

Good soup needs good bread, so we made our own for this class. We revisited the No-Knead Bread recipe from Jim Lahey of Sullivan Street Bakery. See page 76 for the recipe.

Tony had just recently found David Waltuck's wonderful cookbook, *Staff Meals from Chanterelle*, and we fell in love with it. One of the best parts of working in a restaurant kitchen, even (especially) a fancy one, are the staff meals. This book epitomizes that experience for us, so we based a class on it.

Hot Beef Borscht

- 4 lbs beef brisket
- 6 cups beef stock
- vegetable oil for cooking
- 1 large onion, sliced
- 3 large cloves garlic, minced
- 2 ½ quarts chicken stock
- 5 cups peeled and shredded raw beets
- 2/3 cup fresh lemon juice
- 6 cups shredded cabbage
- 2 tbsp sugar
- kosher salt to taste
- black pepper to taste
- sour cream for garnish
- ¼ cup apple cider vinegar

Place brisket in large saucepan with beef stock, so that stock covers the meat. Bring to boil, then reduce to low, simmering partially covered till meat is tender, about 2 hours.

Remove meat, cool until you can handle and cut into 1/2-inch dice. Reserve stock.

Heat oil in a large stock pot over medium heat. Sauté onion and garlic till lightly brown, about 10 minutes. Add the reserved stock and the chicken stock and bring to the boil. Reduce heat to low, add beets and half the lemon juice, simmer uncovered until beets are tender, about 30 minutes. Add beef and cabbage, increase heat and simmer until cabbage is soft and meat is heated through, about 10 minutes more.

Season with the rest of the lemon juice, sugar, vinegar, salt and pepper. Simmer a couple of minutes more to let flavors blend, then serve immediately. Garnish with a dollop of sour cream.

Serves 6-8.

Mushroom Barley Soup

- 5 oz dried porcini mushrooms or dried cepes
- 4 cups hot water
- 3 medium leeks
- 4 tbsp unsalted butter
- 2 carrots, peeled and diced small
- 2 onions cut into ¼" dice
- 2 garlic cloves, minced
- 2 tbsp all-purpose flour
- 10 cups chicken stock
- 2 bay leaves
- ½ cup pearl barley
- salt and pepper to taste

Place dried mushrooms in a bowl and cover with the hot water. Soak at room temperature for half an hour.

Trim all but ½" of the green of the leeks. Split lengthwise and rinse well. Drain and cut into ¼" dice.

Melt butter in a medium saucepan over medium heat. Add carrots, onions, leeks and garlic. Sauté, stirring occasionally, until onions and leeks are wilted, about 10 minutes.

Stir in flour and cook, stirring constantly for 5 minutes. Whisk in chicken stock and raise heat to high.

While soup comes to a boil, lift mushrooms from the soaking liquid with a slotted spoon and set aside. Strain their liquid into the soup through a strainer lined with cheesecloth. Add bay leaves.

Rinse mushrooms and remove any hard or gritty parts. Chop mushrooms coarsely and add to soup.

Add barley and simmer, uncovered, stirring occasionally until barley is tender, about 45 minutes. Remove and discard bay leaves. Season with salt and pepper and serve.

Serves 4-6.

Spiced Honey Cake

- 2 cups honey
- ¾ cup canola oil
- 1 cup strong brewed coffee
- 2 tsp vanilla extract
- 3 ½ cups all-purpose flour
- 1 tbsp ground cinnamon
- 1 tbsp ground ginger
- 1 tsp ground nutmeg
- 1 tsp ground coriander
- 1 tsp baking soda
- 1 tsp baking powder
- 1/2 tsp salt
- 3 large eggs
- ¾ cup sugar
- 2 tbsp sugar
- 2 tbsp unsalted butter
- Bundt or 13x9 cake pan

Preheat oven to 350°F. Oil the cake pan. Combine 1 ½ cups honey, oil, coffee, and vanilla in a small saucepan and heat, stirring constantly, until the mixture is well blended. Remove from heat and let cool.

Place flour, cinnamon, ginger, nutmeg, coriander, baking soda, baking powder, and salt in a large bowl and stir to blend. Place eggs and sugar in a medium bowl and beat with a mixer on medium speed until pale yellow and very thick, 5 minutes. Pour honey mixture into egg mixture and beat until well incorporated. Add dry ingredients. Beat on low speed, stopping the mixer occasionally to scrape down sides.

Spread batter evenly in pan and bake until it springs back when lightly touched and toothpick inserted in the center comes out clean, 40-45 minutes. Cool in pan 5 minutes, then place on a wire rack to cool for 20 minutes. Run a long, sharp knife around the edge of the cake and invert onto a rack to cool while you prepare the glaze. Place remaining honey, sugar, and butter in a small saucepan and bring to a boil over medium heat, stirring constantly. Remove glaze from heat. Use a fork to gently poke holes all over the top of the cake. Brush on the glaze, letting it seep into the holes and down the sides. Serve at room temperature.

An Indian Luncheon, 2/6/08

- **Eggplant Salad**
- **Quick Pan Bread,** *Chapati*
- **Mulligatawney Soup**
- *Dahi Murgh*, **Chicken Curry**

These delightful Indian dishes make a wonderful luncheon. Chapatis are an easy and quick pan bread which make an excellent accompaniment for many Indian meals.

Black Cat's version of Mulligatawney is a huge favorite at the café – in fact a bowl of it is a full meal, but here we used it as a soup before the main curry dish.

Eggplant Salad

- 1 large eggplant
- 1 ½ cups minced onion
- 2 tbsp olive oil
- ½ tsp salt
- 2 tsp mustard seeds
- ¼ tsp cayenne pepper
- 2 tbsp sesame seeds
- ¼ cup lemon juice
- 1 tsp whole cumin seeds
- 2 large garlic cloves, crushed
- water, as needed
- ½ cup plain yoghurt

Cut the eggplant into small cubes, about 3/4". Heat olive oil in a large heavy skillet. Add mustard, sesame and cumin seeds, turn heat up and simmer for a few moments. When seeds begin to pop, add the garlic, onion, salt and cayenne. Stir and cook for 5 minutes, or until the onions soften.

Add the eggplant and stir well. Cover, and reduce heat to medium-low. After about 5 minutes, stir again and add lemon juice. Cover and cook, stirring from time to time, until the eggplant is cooked through. Add water, ¼ cup at a time as needed to prevent sticking. Remove from heat, transfer to a bowl and chill completely. Stir in yoghurt after salad is cold.

Serves 4.

Quick Pan Bread, *Chapati*

- 3 cups fine whole meal flour
- 1 ½ tsp salt or to taste
- 1 tbsp ghee or oil, optional
- 1 cup lukewarm water

Put flour in mixing bowl, reserving ½ cup for rolling chapatis. Mix salt through the flour in the bowl, and then rub in ghee or oil. Add water all at once and mix to a firm but not stiff dough. Knead dough for at least 10 minutes (the more it is kneaded, the lighter the bread will be). Form dough into a ball, cover with clear plastic wrap and stand for 1 hour or longer (if left overnight, the chapatis will be very light.)

Shape dough into balls about the size of a large walnut. Then roll out each one on a lightly floured board to a circular shape as thin as a French crepe. Heat a griddle or heavy frying pan until very hot, and cook the chapatis, starting with those that were rolled first. Put the chapati on griddle and leave for about 1 minute, then turn over and cook a further minute, pressing lightly around the edges with a folded tea towel. As each one is cooked, wrap in a clean tea towel until all are ready. Serve immediately.

Makes about 12.

Black Cat's Mulligatawney

- 2 tbsp olive oil
- 2 stalks celery, chopped
- 1 carrot, peeled and chopped
- 1 onion, peeled and chopped
- 1 2" piece of ginger, peeled and diced
- 1 chili pepper of your choice, seeded and de-veined
- 6 cups water or vegetable or chicken stock (your choice)
- 1 ½ cup red lentils
- salt and pepper to taste
- 1 tbsp curry powder
- 2/3 cup coconut milk
- 2 cups cooked basmati rice
- 1 cup shredded cooked chicken breast
- ½ cup tart raw apple, chopped

For garnish:
- ½ cup toasted coconut
- ¼ bunch fresh cilantro
- 2 ½ tbsp coconut milk
- 1 lime cut in 8 wedges

Sauté onion in oil over medium heat until they are translucent. Add carrot, celery, chili pepper and ginger. Stir in the curry powder to blend and cook for a minute. Pour in the water or stock, add the lentils and bring to a boil. Reduce heat and simmer for 30 minutes.

While the soup is simmering, get the rice cooked (if it isn't already); likewise with the chicken. Then shred the chicken and chop the apples finely. You don't need to peel the apples.

When soup is done, add salt, pepper and more curry powder to taste, then puree. Bring the soup back to a simmer and add the coconut milk. To serve, have big individual serving bowls at the ready. Fill each bowl halfway with soup then spoon some rice into the bowl. Next add some chicken and a spoonful of chopped apple. Sprinkle with fresh cilantro and toasted coconut and serve with a wedge of lime.

Serves 6-8.

Chicken Curry, *Dahi Murgh*

- 3 medium onions peeled and coarsely chopped
- 16 cloves garlic peeled and chopped
- 3 inch piece ginger peeled and chopped
- 6 tbsp oil
- 8 whole cloves garlic
- 10 whole peppercorns
- chili powder to taste
- 2 lbs cut up chicken breasts
- 1 cup and 1/2 cup yoghurt
- salt to taste

Blend onions garlic and ginger into a smooth paste. Heat oil in a large skillet. When it is hot, put in cardamom, cinnamon, cloves and peppercorns. Ten seconds later, add the onion paste and chili powder. Stir-fry for 10 minutes, adjusting heat if necessary until the paste is a rich golden brown. If it seems too thick, add a bit of water.

Now add the chicken pieces, a few at a time and stir them in. Begin to put in the first cup of yoghurt, a tbsp at a time. This should take about 10 minutes. Add the remaining ½ cup of yoghurt, cover and cook on low heat for 10 more minutes, stirring occasionally until chicken is thoroughly cooked.

Serve with chapati bread.

Serves 4-6.

Italian Tarts, Sweet and Savory, 3/2/09

- **Fresh Artichoke Tart, *Torta di Carciofi***
- **Potato and Egg Cake, *Tortino di Patate alle Uova***

- **Almond Tart, *Crostata di Mandorle***

Fresh Artichoke Tart, *Torta di Carciofi*

Pastry
- 1 ½ cups all purpose unbleached flour
- ½ cup cake flour

- ¼ tsp each of salt and pepper
- 10 tbsp unsalted butter
- 8 tbsp cold water
- 1 egg, beaten, for glaze

Filling
- 6 large artichokes
- 2 large lemons
- 1 ½ cups water
- 2 oz thinly sliced pancetta, chopped
- 2 tbsp extra-virgin olive oil
- 1 onion, minced
- 3 tbsp minced carrot
- salt and pepper to taste

- 1 tbsp shredded lemon zest
- 1 large clove garlic, minced
- 8 tbsp minced fresh basil leaves, or 4 tsp dried basil
- ½ cup water
- 2 tsp fresh lemon juice
- 1 cup freshly grated Parmigiano-Reggiano cheese

Grease a 10- inch fluted tart pan with removable bottom. Combine the flour, salt and pepper in a food processor or mixing bowl and blend. Cut in the butter until the mixture resembles small peas. Process a few seconds in the machine, then sprinkle the cold water over the dough. Use the on/off pulse to blend the dough just until it forms clumps. Do not mix so much that the dough forms a ball as that will toughen it. Gather the dough into a ball, wrap in plastic wrap, and chill about 30 minutes. Roll out half the dough to less than 1/8 inch thick, and fit it into the tart pan, leaving a 1 inch border. Roll out the remaining dough to form a large circle of the same thickness. Spread it on a foil-covered baking sheet. Chill both pastry pieces 30 minutes or up to 24 hours.

Halve both lemons and squeeze the juice of three halves into a medium bowl. Add the water. As you cut the artichoke, keep rubbing the surface with the remaining lemon half to keep them from darkening. Remove the stem, and leaves, and scoop out the fuzzy choke with a spoon. Immediately immerse the bottom in the lemon water. Drain the artichoke bottoms, pat them dry and cut into bite-size chunks. Heat the pancetta and oil over medium heat. Sauté pancetta 2 -3 minutes to give up its fat. Raise heat to medium-high, add artichoke pieces and sauté, uncovered, 4 minutes, or until they begin to color. Stir in the onion, carrot, and a light sprinkling of salt and pepper. Cook, stirring frequently, 4 minutes, or until the onion has browned and the artichokes are golden.

Reduce heat, add lemon zest, garlic, and basil, and cook 30 seconds. Add the water and bring to a boil, scraping up the brown bits from the bottom of the skillet. Cover and simmer 3-4 minutes, or until artichokes are slightly softened. Uncover and cook down the juices 1 minute, or until they form a moist glaze on the bottom of the skillet. The artichoke should still be a bit crisp. Remove from heat and allow to cool. When cool, season to taste with lemon juice.

Preheat oven to 425°F. Remove pastry from the refrigerator and spread the filling in it. Sprinkle liberally with the cheese, and top with the sheet of dough, pressing the edges together. Brush the crust with the beaten egg, and pierce with a fork. Bake in the lower third of the oven 15 minutes. Lower the heat to 375°F and bake another 25 minutes, or until golden brown. Serve hot or warm.

Serves 8.

Potato and Egg Cake, *Tortino di Patate alle Uova*

- 2 lb unpeeled boiling potatoes
- 4 oz unsalted butter
- ½ cup milk
- 6 oz freshly grated parmesan cheese

- 2 large eggs plus 6 large yolks
- 12 paper thin slices fontina cheese
- 12 anchovy fillets in oil, drained
- ½ tsp each salt and pepper

Put the potatoes in a large saucepan, cover with water and bring to a boil. Boil for about 30 minutes until tender, then drain. When cool enough to handle, peel and mash while still hot. Leave in the pan and beat in half the butter, the milk and parmesan and heat over a low heat for about 10 minutes, stirring all the time with a wooden spoon. Add salt and pepper. Let cool completely, then add 2 whole eggs, beating them well.

Meanwhile, preheat the oven to 350°F. Butter a baking dish and spoon the potato mixture into it. Smooth with a knife and make 6 indentations, large enough to hold the egg yolks. Place a slice of fontina cheese in each indentation, dotting the rest of the butter on top. Cook in the oven for about 20 minutes, or until barely golden. Fill the indentations with the yolks and cross each yolk with the anchovy fillets. Top with the rest of the fontina slices.

Cook for a further 5 minutes or until the fontina starts to melt, but the yolks remain runny. Serve immediately.

Serves 6-8.

Almond Tart, *Crostata di Mandorle*

Pastry
- 1 1/4 cups all purpose flour
- 3 tbsp sugar
- ½ tsp salt
- grated zest of 1 orange
- 8 tbsp cold unsalted butter, cut into bits
- 1 egg lightly beaten
- 1 tsp vanilla

In a large bowl combine the flour, sugar, salt and zest. Blend in the butter until the mixture resembles coarse meal. Add the egg and vanilla and mix until incorporated. Gather into a ball, wrap in plastic wrap and chill at least 1 hour.

Roll out the dough 1/8" thick on a floured surface. Fit it into a 9" pan with a removable fluted rim, and crimp the edge. Chill the shell for 30 minutes.

Filling
- 3 large eggs
- 1/4 cup granulated sugar
- 8 oz almond paste
- ¾ cup raspberry jam
- ½ cup all-purpose flour
- 1/3 cup sliced almonds
- confectioners' sugar, for dusting

Spread the jam on the bottom of the shell. In the bowl of an electric mixer, beat the eggs until they are foamy and beat in the granulated sugar gradually. Crumble the almond paste into the egg mixture, and beat until it is combined well. Fold in the flour gently but thoroughly. Spread the mixture evenly over the jam and sprinkle it with the almonds.

Bake the tart in the lower third of a preheated 350°F oven for 35 to 40 minutes, or until it is golden and firm in the center. Let it cool in the pan on a rack for 10 minutes. Remove the rim, let the tart cool completely on the rack, and dust with confectioner's sugar.

Two Soups and Two Bread Puddings, 3/11/08

- **Vanessa's Famous Local Corn Chowder**
- **Fresh Asparagus Soup**

- **Rum Raisin Bread Pudding**
- **Chocolate Silk Bread Pudding**

Vanessa's Famous Corn Chowder

Made with the excellent local corn, this has become a classic summer favorite at the Black Cat. The local onions and potatoes are also a big part of it. We use an extra-sharp cheddar from Cuba (NY that is!) We only serve it in late August and September at the Café, when all the ingredients are local and fresh.

- 8 oz applewood-smoked bacon, chopped
- ¾ cup olive oil
- 6 cups chopped yellow onions (about 4 large onions)
- 4 tbsp butter
- ½ cup flour
- 2 tsp kosher salt
- 1 tsp black pepper
- ½ tsp ground turmeric
- 12 cups chicken stock
- 6 cups medium-diced white potatoes, unpeeled
- 10 cups corn kernels, fresh (about 10-12 ears)
- 2 cups half-and-half
- 8 oz sharp white cheddar, grated

In a large stockpot over medium-high heat, cook the bacon and olive oil until the bacon is crisp, about 5 minutes. Remove bacon with a slotted spoon and set aside. Reduce heat, add onions and butter to the fat, and cook 10 minutes, or until the onions are translucent. Stir in flour, salt, pepper, and turmeric and cook for 3 minutes. Add chicken stock and potatoes, bring to a boil, and simmer uncovered for 15 minutes, until the potatoes are tender.

Add the corn to the soup, and then add the half-and-half and cheddar. Cook for 5 more minutes, until the cheese is melted. Season to taste and serve hot with a garnish of bacon.

Serves 8-10.

Fresh Asparagus Soup

- 2 lb fresh green asparagus
- 1 large onion, chopped
- 4 tbsp unsalted butter
- 5-6 cups chicken broth
- ½ cup heavy cream
- ¾ tsp fresh lemon juice

Cut tips from asparagus and reserve for garnish. Snap off the tough bottoms, then cut the remaining asparagus into ½ inch pieces.

Cook onion in half the butter in a 4-quart pot over moderately low heat, stirring, until softened. Add asparagus pieces, salt and pepper to taste, and cook, stirring, 5 minutes. Add 5 cups broth and simmer, covered, until asparagus is very tender, 15-20 minutes.

Cook asparagus tips in boiling salted water until just tender, 3-4 minutes, and then drain. Puree soup in batches in a blender until smooth, transferring to a bowl and return to pan. Stir in cream, then add more broth to thin the soup to desired consistency. Season with salt and pepper. Bring soup to a boil and whisk in remaining butter.

Add lemon juice and garnish with the asparagus tips.

Serves 6.

Chocolate Silk Bread Pudding

- 4 cups milk
- ½ stick butter in small pieces
- 5 oz unsweetened chocolate
- 2 large eggs
- ½ cup sugar
- 1 tsp pure vanilla extract
- 1 tsp ground cinnamon
- ¼ tsp salt
- 2 cups soft fresh bread crumbs

Preheat oven to 325°F, with rack in center. Butter a 1.5 quart shallow baking dish.

In a medium saucepan, combine the milk, butter and chocolate. Bring to boil over medium low heat, and stir occasionally, until butter and chocolate melt.

Meanwhile, in a large bowl, whisk the eggs, sugar, vanilla, cinnamon and salt. Add bread crumbs and stir in the hot milk mixture. Pour into prepared baking dish.

Bake until the pudding is set and kind of wobbly, but not liquid in the center, about 45-60 minutes. Let cool on a wire rack.

Serve the pudding, slightly warm or cold, with whipped cream if you like.

Serves 6.

Rum Raisin Bread Pudding

- ¼ cup butter, melted
- 1 cup dark raisins
- ½ cup dark rum
- 4-6 slices sturdy white bread
- 2 cups white bread, cubed

- 2 cups milk
- 2 cups cream
- 1 tbsp vanilla
- 7 large eggs
- ¾ cup sugar

Combine raisins and rum. Allow to marinate for 1 hour. Preheat oven to 350°F.

Bring milk, cream and vanilla to a simmer in a saucepan. Turn off heat and allow to cool for 5 minutes. In a large bowl combine eggs and sugar, mix well. Slowly incorporate cooled cream into eggs while whisking until well combined.

Brush baking dish with melted butter. Add cubed bread and rum soaked raisins. Pour in custard. Brush bread slices with butter and place on top gently pressing down to absorb custard. Drizzle remaining butter over bread slices.

Place filled baking dish in a water bath. Bake for 45-50 minutes at 350°F until golden brown and set. Cool for 10-15 minutes before serving, with Vanilla ice cream if you like.

Serves 10-12.

Two Hearty Soups, 3/21/07

- **Mulligatawney**
- **Minestrone**

This class featured two marvelous hearty soups. You can see our recipe for **Black Cat's Mulligatawney** on page 57.

Mulligatawney is usually a curry-flavored soup of Anglo-Indian origin. A literal translation from the Tamil is "pepper water". Despite the name, pepper itself is not a vital ingredient and there are many variations on the recipe. Black Cat's version is a wonderful complex composed soup based on a red-lentil puree.

The word "minestrone" is from the Italian word for "soup" – but because it is usually made with whatever is in season, it has become a synonym for "hodgepodge".

Minestrone

- ½ lb dried white beans, soaked overnight
- 1 tsp olive oil
- 1/4 lb salt pork, in small dice
- 2 garlic cloves, chopped finely
- 1 onion, chopped
- 1 leek, washed and diced
- 2 tsp parsley, chopped
- 1 tsp basil, chopped
- 1 tbsp tomato paste
- 3 tomatoes, peeled, seeded and chopped
- 3 celery stalks, chopped
- 3 carrots, sliced
- 2 potatoes, diced
- 2 turnips, peeled and diced
- ¼ small cabbage, shredded
- 2 zucchini, diced
- 1 ½ quarts water
- salt and black pepper taste
- 1 cup elbow macaroni
- 6 tbsp grated Parmesan cheese

Drain beans and boil in 3 quarts of water for about 1 hour or until tender.

Place olive oil in a large pot, and add salt pork, garlic, onions, leek, parsley and basil, and brown lightly. Add tomato paste thinned with a little water and cook 5 minutes. Add tomatoes, celery, carrots, potatoes, turnip, cabbage, zucchini, water, salt and pepper.

Cook slowly, 45 minutes to an hour. Add the beans. Add the macaroni and cook 10 minutes or until tender.

Let the soup cool and rest for flavors to develop, 20 minutes. Correct seasoning, re-warm and pour into heated bowls. Serve immediately, garnished with grated Parmesan.

Serves 6.

Black Cat Café Favorites, 3/23/09

- **James Beard's French Toast**
- **Carrot-Ginger Soup**
- **Tuscan-style Grilled Chicken Melt**
- **Coconut Cake**

This wonderful French Toast recipe is based on one Marion Cunningham says was reportedly served on the Santa Fe Railroad, and popularized by James Beard. The corn flakes add a wonderful sweetness and crunch. It is a huge favorite at the café.

When we first opened the Café a regular feature was the Barefoot Contessa's coconut cupcakes, but they tended to get dry and dense in the refrigerated case, so we turned it into this great coconut cake, which kept better.

Our Carrot and Ginger soup is inspired by a recipe in Bernard Clayton's amazing soup book. And the Tuscan sandwich, another big seller, came about from experimenting with Panini sandwiches.

Carrot and Ginger Soup

- 2 tbsp butter
- 2 onions, peeled and coarsely chopped
- 1 ½ lbs carrots, peeled and sliced
- 3 tbsp shredded fresh ginger
- 6 cups chicken stock
- 1 ½ cups cream
- 1 tsp salt or to taste
- large pinch pepper

Melt butter in a medium saucepan and cook the onions uncovered over low heat until translucent, about 15 minutes. Add carrots and shredded ginger, cover and cook over medium-low heat for 20 minutes. Bring chicken stock to a simmer in a separate saucepan. Add to the carrot mixture and boil gently over medium heat for about 20 minutes or until the carrots are fork tender. Remove from heat and process in a food processor or blender. Stir in the cream, and then add salt and pepper to taste. Reheat the soup gently, but do not let it boil; serve warm (it shouldn't be too hot.)

Tuscan-style Grilled Chicken Melt

- 4 tsp prepared pesto
- 2 ciabatta rolls
- 2 skinless boneless chicken breasts, grilled
- 4 slices good mozzarella
- 3 baby artichoke hearts, quartered
- 1 ½ small ripe tomatoes, thinly sliced
- 1 ½ cups baby greens

Split the ciabattas and spread bottom halves with pesto. Slice chicken breasts diagonally into 4 or 5 strips and place on the ciabatta. Cover with artichoke and tomato, and top with mozzarella slices.   Melt face up under a cheese melter if you have one. If you don't have a cheese melter, the sandwiches can be assembled and placed in the panini grill for a little longer. Once cheese melts, place top half of ciabatta on and place in a panini grill for 2-3 minutes.

Remove, reopen sandwiches and stuff with mixed greens. Slice in half and serve.

Serves 2.

Coconut Layer Cake

- 3/4 lb unsalted butter at room temperature
- 2 cups sugar
- 5 extra large eggs at room temperature
- 1 ½ tsp pure vanilla extract
- 1 ½ tsp almond extract
- 3 cups all-purpose flour
- 1 tsp baking powder
- ½ tsp baking soda
- ½ tsp kosher salt
- 1 cup milk
- 4 oz sweetened flaked coconut for cake, plus 8 oz for garnish
- 2 9" pans and parchment paper

Preheat oven to 350°F. Line two 9" cake pans with parchment paper. Cream the butter and sugar on medium to high speed for 3-5 minutes.

Crack eggs into a small bowl. With mixer on medium speed, add eggs one at a time, scraping down bowl once during mixing. Add vanilla and almond extracts and mix well. In a separate bowl, sift together dry ingredients. With mixer on low, alternately add dry ingredients and milk to batter.

Mix until just combined and then fold in the coconut. Pour batter into pans, smoothing tops. Bake in center of oven 40-50 minutes until tops are brown and cake tester comes out clean. Cool on baking rack for 30 minutes before removing cakes from pans.

Prepare frosting:
- 1 lb soft cream cheese
- ½ lb unsalted butter
- ¾ tsp pure vanilla extract
- ¼ tsp almond extract
- 1 lb confectioners' sugar
- 6 ounces flaked coconut

Mix cream cheese, butter, vanilla, and almond extract. Add confectioners' sugar and mix until just smooth (don't whip). Assemble cake by placing one layer, top side down, and spreading it with frosting. Place second layer on top of the first. Frost the top and sides. Sprinkle cake lightly with shredded coconut. Serve at room temperature.

James Beard's French Toast

- 2 eggs
- ½ cup cream
- 1 tsp vanilla
- 2 cups lightly crushed cornflakes

- 2 slices sturdy white bread
- ¼ cup (more or less) vegetable oil
- cinnamon and powdered sugar for garnish

One of the most popular breakfasts at the Café is this fabulous version of French Toast. The crispy crunch of the cornflake coating before the tender inside covered with warmed local maple syrup is irresistibly delicious.

With a fork, whisk together eggs, cream and vanilla in a bowl big enough to dip the bread slices in. Crush the cornflakes and place in a second bowl.

Heat oil in a large non-stick pan (or on a flat-top if you have one.) While the oil is heating dip the bread in the egg mixture and then in the cornflake bowl. Press cornflakes onto the bread slices to coat the bread well on both sides.

When the oil is hot, fry the coated bread slices on medium heat flipping once until both sides are golden brown. Blot off extra oil with a paper towel. Cut in half and arrange 3 halves on each plate. Dust with cinnamon and confectioner's sugar.

Serve immediately with warm maple syrup.

Serves 2.

Day Classes - Baking and Desserts

No-knead Bread, 2/13/07

Jim Lahey of Sullivan Street Bakery in NY started a rage of bread-making with Mark Bittman of the NY Times' "No-Knead Bread" article on November 8, 2006. It was the #1 most emailed NYT article that week. Countless follow-up articles including one by Bittman on December 6, 2006, "No Kneading, but Some Fine-Tuning."

We've been using it ever since and have modified it a little for our own versions.

Basic Recipe, White Boule

- 3 ½ cups white bread flour, more for dusting
- ¼ tsp instant yeast
- 2 cups tepid water
- 2 tsp salt
- cornmeal for dusting
- 4-5 quart oven-proof pot

In a large bowl combine flour, yeast and salt. Add the water, and stir until blended; dough will be shaggy and sticky. Cover bowl with plastic wrap. Let dough rest for 12-18 hours at room temperature.

Dough is ready when its surface is dotted with bubbles. Lightly flour a work surface and place dough on it; sprinkle it with a little more flour and fold it over on itself once or twice. Using just enough flour to keep dough from sticking to work surface or to your fingers, gently and quickly shape dough into a ball. Generously coat a cotton towel (not terry cloth) with flour, wheat bran or cornmeal; put dough seam side down on towel and dust with more flour and some cornmeal.

Cover with another cotton towel and let rise for about 2 hours. Note that when it is ready, the dough will be more than double in size and will not readily spring back when poked with a finger.

About a half-hour before dough is ready, heat oven to 500°F. Put a 4-5 quart heavy covered pot (cast iron, enamel, Pyrex or ceramic) in the oven as it heats to temperature. When the dough is ready, carefully remove pot from oven. Slide your hand under towel and turn dough over into pot, seam side up; it may look like a mess, but that is fine.

Shake pan once or twice if dough is unevenly distributed; it will straighten out as it bakes. Cover with lid and bake 30 minutes, then remove lid and bake another 15 to 20 minutes, until loaf is beautifully browned. Cool on a rack.

Two Scones and Two Biscotti, 1/31/07

- Raisin Scones
- Candied Ginger Scones

- Double-Chocolate Walnut Biscotti
- Tuscan Almond Biscotti

These two scones are staples at the café, outselling all others by a huge margin. They are very different but both uncommonly moist and flavorful for scones.

The biscotti recipes are two of our favorites, and wonderful with a cup of our Black Pearl espresso or our dark Ethiopian-Sumatran blend – or any coffee of your choice.

Raisin Scones

- 4 cups all-purpose flour
- 2 tbsp sugar, plus extra for sprinkling
- 2 tbsp baking powder
- ¾ pound cold unsalted butter, diced
- 1 tsp salt
- 4 extra-large eggs, lightly beaten
- 1 cup cold heavy cream
- 1 cup jumbo raisins
- 1 egg beaten with 2 tbsp water

Preheat oven to 400°F.

In the bowl of an electric mixer fitted with a paddle attachment, combine 4 cups of flour, 2 tbsp sugar, baking powder, and salt. Blend in the cold butter at the lowest speed and mix until the butter is in pea-sized pieces.

Combine the eggs and heavy cream and quickly add them to the flour and butter mixture. Combine until just blended. Add raisins to the dough, and mix quickly. The dough may be a bit sticky.

Dump the dough out onto a well-floured surface and be sure it is well combined. Flour your hands and a rolling pin and roll the dough 3/4-inch thick. You should see lumps of butter in the dough. Cut into squares with a 4-inch plain or fluted cutter, and then cut them in half diagonally to make triangles.

Place on a baking sheet lined with parchment paper. Brush the tops with egg wash. Sprinkle with sugar and bake for 20 to 25 minutes, until the outsides are crisp and the insides are fully baked.

Makes 8 scones.

Candied Ginger Scones

- 3" round cutter
- 2 ½ cups pastry flour
- ½ cup granulated sugar
- 1 tbsp baking powder
- 1 tbsp finely chopped lemon zest
- 6 oz unsalted butter, diced
- 1 cup candied ginger, diced
- ¾ cup heavy cream plus extra for brushing tops before baking

Adjust oven rack to middle position and preheat oven to 400°F.

With food processor or mixer, combine flour, sugar and baking powder, and pulse or mix on low to incorporate. Add lemon zest and butter then pulse on and off or mix on low until mixture is pale yellow and the consistency of a fine meal.

Transfer into a large mixing bowl and mix in 2/3 cups of the ginger. Make a well in the center and pour in 1/2 cup of the cream. Using one hand, draw in the dry ingredients until just combined. If mixture seems dry, add the remaining cream.

Wash and dry hands and dust with flour. Turn the dough out onto a lightly floured surface and gently knead a few times to gather it into a ball. Roll or pat dough into a circle about 1/4 " thick. Cut out 3" circles, as close as possible, keeping trimmings intact. Gather scraps, pat and press pieces back together and cut circles out of remaining dough.

Place scones 1" apart on a parchment-lined baking sheet. Brush the tops with the remaining cream and sprinkle with the remaining ginger. Bake 12-16 minutes, or until the surface cracks and they are slightly brown.

Makes 8 scones.

Double-Chocolate Walnut Biscotti

- 2 cups all-purpose flour
- 1/3 cup unsweetened cocoa powder
- 1 tsp baking soda
- 1 tsp salt
- 6 tbsp unsalted butter, softened
- 1 cup granulated sugar
- 2 large eggs
- 1 ¼ cup walnuts, chopped
- ½ cup semisweet choc chips
- 1 tbsp confectioners' sugar

Place rack in middle of oven and preheat to 350°F. Cover a large baking sheet with parchment paper. Mix together flour, cocoa, baking soda, salt in a bowl. Beat together butter and granulated sugar in a large bowl with an electric mixer at high speed until combined, about 30 seconds. Add eggs and beat until well-combined. Stir in flour mixture; dough will be stiff. Stir in walnuts and chocolate chips.

Halve dough. With floured hands, form dough into 2 slightly flattened 12x2 inch logs on baking sheet, about 3" apart. Sprinkle with confectioners' sugar.

Bake logs until slightly firm to the touch about 35 minutes. Cool on a baking sheet on a rack for 5 minutes leaving the oven on.

Transfer logs to a cutting board. With a serrated knife cut diagonally into 3/4" thick slices. Arrange sliced biscotti cut sides down on baking sheet. Bake until crisp about 10 minutes. Transfer to racks to cool.

Makes about 2 dozen.

Tuscan Almond Biscotti

- 2 ½ cups all-purpose flour
- 1 tsp baking powder
- ½ tsp baking soda
- 1 tsp salt
- 4 large eggs
- ¾ cup sugar
- 1 tbsp grated orange zest
- 2 tsp vanilla extract
- 1 ½ cup toasted almonds, coarsely chopped

Preheat oven to 325°F.

Cover a large cookie sheet with parchment paper. Sift together flour baking powder, baking soda and salt. In a large bowl beat eggs and sugar until light and foamy. Beat in orange zest and vanilla. Stir in the dry ingredients, and then stir in the almonds.

Halve dough. With floured hands, form dough into 2 slightly flattened 14x2 inch logs on baking sheet, about 4" apart. Smooth tops and sides with rubber spatula.

Bake logs until firm to the touch and golden about 30 minutes. Cool on a baking sheet on a rack for 10 minutes leaving the oven on, and reduce temperature to 275°F. Transfer logs to a cutting board. With a large heavy chef's knife cut diagonally into 1/2" thick slices.

Stand sliced biscotti about 1/2" apart on baking sheet. Bake until lightly toasted about 30 minutes. Transfer to racks to cool.

Makes about 2 dozen.

Muffins and Quick Breads, 2/5/08

- **Raw Apple Muffins**
- **Carrot Date Muffins**

- **Quick Beer Bread**
- **Wheat Quick Bread**

Raw Apple Muffins

- 4 cups peeled apples, diced
- 1 cup sugar
- 2 eggs
- ½ cup vegetable oil
- 2 tsp vanilla extract

- 2 cups flour
- 2 tsp baking soda
- 2 tsp cinnamon
- 1 tsp salt
- 1 cup jumbo raisins
- 1 cup walnuts

Preheat oven to 350° F. Line 12 large muffin cups with paper.

We love to use Honey Crisps for these, but they work fine with Granny Smith or Macoun apples.

Whisk eggs, oil, sugar and vanilla, then add flour, baking soda, cinnamon and salt and stir together. This is going to make a very stiff batter. Then add the apples in. Next mix in the raisins and walnuts.

Put into the muffin tins using your hands. Bake about 35 minutes or until a toothpick inserted in center comes out clean.   Makes 12 muffins.

Carrot Date Muffins

- 2 large eggs
- ½ cup vegetable oil
- ¼ cup molasses
- ¾ cup sugar
- 2 cups grated carrots
- 2/3 cup chopped dates

- 1 cup flour
- ¾ tsp baking powder
- ¾ tsp baking soda
- ½ salt
- 1 ½ tsp cinnamon
- 4 nice dates cut in half for garnish

In separate bowls, mix the wet ingredients (on the left above) together first, then mix the dry ingredients together. Now, mix the wet and dry ingredients together to create the batter. Spoon muffin batter evenly between the muffin cups. Top each muffin with half a date and a generous sprinkle of sugar. Bake 25 minutes until firm on top. Makes 8.

Quick Beer Bread

- 3 cups self-rising flour
- 3 tbsp sugar
- 12 oz can beer, your choice
- ½ cup melted butter

Combine flour and sugar. Add beer and mix well. Pour into a well-greased loaf pan and bake at 350°F.

After 15 minutes, drizzle 1/3 of the butter over the bread. After a second 15 minutes, drizzle the second third of the butter over the bread. Just before the bread is done, drizzle the remaining butter over the bread. Remove from the oven and cool on rack before turning out

Quick Whole Wheat and Molasses Bread

- oil or butter for greasing pan
- 1 2/3 cups buttermilk or plain yoghurt
- 2 ¼   cups whole wheat flour
- 1/3 cup cornmeal
- 1 tsp salt
- 1 tsp baking soda
- ½ cup molasses.

Preheat oven to 325°F. Grease an 8x4-inch loaf pan, preferably nonstick. Mix together the dry ingredients. Stir molasses into buttermilk or yoghurt. Stir liquid into dry ingredients (just enough to combine) then pour into loaf pan.

Bake until firm and a toothpick inserted into center comes out clean, 45 minutes to 1 hour. Cool on a rack for 15 minutes before removing from pan.

Winter Fruit Desserts, 2/12/08

- **Vanessa's Huguenot Torte**
- **Apple Crostata**
- **Rote Grütze, German Berry Compote**

A note about Honey Crisp apples:

These amazing "new" apples have spoiled us and now have become the standard by which we measure and compare all other eating apples. Refreshing and a bit tart, yet sweet and with a lovely finish. A fairly new hybrid of Macoun and Honey Gold (1974) and only released in 1991. They are thin skinned, sweet, with a lovely outer pinkish green hue and cream colored flesh, and come in two grades: one smallish and one large sized apple that can weigh a pound each.

Honey Crisp apples have a signature high water content that makes for an ultra-crisp bite. Because of its high water content this is not the best apple for baking everything, but works beautifully in our Raw Apple Muffins (see page 84), the Crostata and even the Huguenot Torte.

Mixed Berry Compote, *Rote Grütze*

- 2 ½ lb. frozen mixed berries (strawberries, raspberries, blackberries, blueberries etc.)
- ½ cup sugar
- 2 cups plus 4 tbsp of 100% fruit juice, including the reserved juice
- 2 ½ tbsp cornstarch

Thaw berries and reserve juice. Mix together cornstarch and 4 tbsp of the juice and set aside. Pour the rest of the juice into a saucepan, stir in sugar and bring to a boil. Remove from heat, stir in cornstarch, return to heat and bring to a boil again. Remove from heat, stir in more sugar if needed and carefully stir in berries. Cool before storing in refrigerator. Serve chilled with vanilla ice cream or plain heavy cream.

Huguenot Apple Torte

- 4 large eggs
- 3 cups sugar
- 8 tbsp sifted flour
- 5 tsp baking powder
- ½ tsp salt
- 3 tsp + 1 tsp vanilla
- 2 cups peeled and coarsely chopped NY apples (we prefer Honey Crisps when available, otherwise Granny Smiths)
- 2 cups chopped walnuts
- 2 ½ cups cream for whipping
- ¼ cup confectioners' sugar

Beat eggs with sugar until pale-yellow. Sift flour, baking powder and salt. Fold flour mixture into eggs and combine well. Stir in chopped apples, walnuts and vanilla. Divide in half and pour into two 9x13" baking pans lined with aluminum foil and well buttered. Bake at 350 °F for 35-45 minutes until set. Let cool. Whip cream, 1 tsp vanilla and confectioners' sugar until thick.

Using the aluminum foil, remove cakes from pans, turn them upside down and remove foil. Place one cake right side up and cover with freshly whipped cream, and then top with the second cake. Dust with confectioner's sugar and serve.

Apple Crostata

- 1 cup all-purpose flour
- 2 tbsp granulated sugar
- ½ tsp kosher salt
- ¼ pound (1 stick) very cold unsalted butter, diced
- 2 tbsp ice water

Make the pastry first. Place flour, sugar, and salt in the bowl of a food processor fitted with a steel blade. Pulse a few times to combine. Add the butter and pulse 12 to 15 times, or until the butter is the size of peas. With the motor running, add the ice water all at once through the feed tube. Keep hitting the pulse button to combine, but stop the machine just before the dough becomes a solid mass. Turn the dough onto a well-floured board and form into a disk. Wrap with plastic and refrigerate for at least 1 hour. Preheat the oven to 450 F.

- 1½ pounds Honey Crisp apples, peeled
- 1 tsp grated orange zest
- ¼ cup flour
- ¼ cup granulated sugar
- ½ tsp kosher salt
- ½ tsp ground cinnamon
- 4 tbsp cold unsalted butter, diced

For the filling, peel, core, and cut the apples into eighths. Cut each wedge into 3 chunks. Toss the chunks with the orange zest. Flour a rolling pin and roll the pastry into an 11-inch circle on a lightly floured surface. Transfer it to a baking sheet. Cover the tart dough with the apple chunks leaving a 1 ½ - inch border.

Combine the flour, sugar, salt, cinnamon, and allspice in the bowl of a food processor fitted with a steel blade. Add the butter and pulse until the mixture is crumbly. Pour into a bowl and rub it with your fingers until it starts holding together. Sprinkle evenly on the apples. Gently fold the border over the apples to enclose the dough, pleating it to make a circle. Bake for 20-25 minutes, until the crust is golden and the apples are tender. Allow to cool. Serve warm or at room temperature.

Serves 6-8.

Elegant Chocolate Class, 2/13/08

- **Queen Mother's Cake**
- **Flourless Chocolate Cake**
- **Hand-made Chocolate Truffles**

Queen Mother's Cake is an elegant, elaborate cake from Maida Heatter, who says that she originally got the recipe in 1962 from a food column in *The New York Herald Tribune* about Jan Smeterlin, the eminent Polish pianist, who loved to cook. When the Queen Mother was invited to tea at his home they served to her and she loved it and asked for the recipe. The, the story goes that the Queen Mother served it often at her royal parties, including the time she invited the Smeterlins.

Vanessa's version is little simpler than that one, but it still comes out wonderfully!

Hand-made Chocolate Truffles

- 1 pound good bittersweet chocolate, like Callebaut
- 1 cup heavy cream
- 2 tbsp liqueur (like Grand Marnier)
- 1 tbsp prepared coffee
- 1 tsp good vanilla extract
- confectioners' sugar for dusting
- Dutch process cocoa powder for dusting

Chop chocolate finely with a sharp knife. Place in a heat-proof mixing bowl. Heat cream in a small saucepan until it just boils. Turn off the heat and allow the cream to sit for 20 seconds.

Pour cream into bowl with chocolate. With a wire whisk, slowly stir the cream and chocolates together until chocolate is completely melted. Whisk in the liqueur, if using, coffee, and vanilla.

Set aside at room temperature for 1 hour.

With 2 teaspoons, spoon round balls of the chocolate mixture onto a baking sheet lined with parchment paper. Roll each ball of chocolate in your hands to roughly make it round. Roll in confectioners' sugar, cocoa powder, or both. Keep refrigerated, but serve at room temperature.

Makes 12- 16 truffles.

Flourless Chocolate Cake

This version, our eldest son Sebastian's favorite cake, is outstandingly dense and rich because, in addition to the structure the eggs give, it substitutes cocoa powder for the flour. The little secret (which there is no need to share with your guests) is that it is also one of the easiest of all cakes to put together.

- 9 ounces good bittersweet chocolate (not unsweetened), chopped, like Callebaut
- ½ lb unsalted butter
- 1 ½ cups sugar
- ½ tsp salt
- 6 large eggs
- 1 cup unsweetened cocoa powder, plus additional for dusting
- 10-inch spring-form pan

Put a rack in middle of oven and preheat oven to 350°F. Butter pan, line bottom with a round of parchment or wax paper, and butter paper.

Melt chocolate with butter in a medium metal bowl set over a saucepan of barely simmering water, stirring until smooth. Remove bowl from heat and whisk in sugar. Add eggs one at a time, whisking well after each addition. Sift cocoa powder over chocolate and whisk until just combined, and add salt.

Pour batter into pan. Bake until top has formed a thin crust and wooden pick or skewer inserted in center of cake comes out with moist crumbs adhering, 35 to 40 minutes. Cool cake in pan on a rack for 10 minutes, and then remove side of pan. Invert cake onto a plate and re-invert onto rack to cool completely.

Dust cake with cocoa powder before serving.

Serves 6-8.

Queen Mother's Cake

- 6 oz (scant 1 ½ cups) almonds, blanched or not based on your preference
- 6 oz semisweet chocolate, cut in small pieces
- ¾ cup granulated sugar

- 6 oz (1 ½ sticks) unsalted butter
- 6 eggs, separated
- 1/8 tsp salt
- 1 tsp lemon juice
- fine, dry bread crumbs

Toast the almonds in a 350°F oven for 12-15 minutes, shaking the pan a few times, until the almonds are lightly colored. Set aside to cool.

Adjust a rack one-third up in the oven and raise the temperature to 375°F. Butter a 9 x 3-inch spring form pan and line the bottom with a round of baking pan liner paper. Butter the paper. Dust all over with fine dry, bread crumbs, invert over paper, and tap lightly to shake out excess. Set aside.

- ½ cup whipping cream
- 8 oz semisweet chocolate, cut in small pieces

- 2 tsp powdered (not granular) instant espresso or coffee

Start the icing. Place chocolate in a small double boiler on moderate heat. Cover until partially melted, then uncover and stir until just melted and smooth. Remove top and cool to room temperature. Place almonds and ¼ cup of the sugar in a food processor. Process until nuts are fine and powdery.

In the large bowl of an electric mixer beat the butter until soft. Add ¼ cup of the sugar and beat to mix. Add egg yolks one at a time, beating and scraping the sides of the bowl until smooth. On low speed, add chocolate and beat until mixed. Then add processed almonds and beat, scraping the bowl, until incorporated.

In the large bowl of the mixer, with clean beaters, beat the egg whites with the salt and lemon juice, starting on low speed and increasing gradually. When the whites barely hold a soft shape, reduce the speed a bit and gradually add the remaining ¼ cup sugar. Then, on high speed, continue to beat until the whites hold a straight point when the beaters are slowly raised. Do not overbeat. Stir a large spoonful of the whites into the chocolate mixture to soften it a bit. Then, in 3 additions, fold in the whites. Do not fold thoroughly until the last addition and do not handle any more than necessary. Turn mixture into the prepared pan. Bake for 20 minutes at 375°F and then reduce to 350°F and bake for another 50 minutes. The cake should remain soft and moist in the center.

Remove cake pan from the oven and place it on a wet towel. Let stand for an hour, then release and remove the sides of the pan. Now let the cake stand until it is completely cool. The cake will sink a little in the middle. Use a long, thin, sharp knife and cut the top level. Brush away loose crumbs. Place a rack or a small board over the cake and carefully invert. Remove the bottom of the pan and the paper lining. The cake is now upside down; this is the way it will be iced.

Place four strips of baking pan-liner paper around the edges of a cake plate. Carefully transfer the cake to the plate, making be sure that the cake is touching the paper all around.

Now, finish the icing. Scald the cream in a medium saucepan over moderate heat until it begins to form small bubbles around the edges or a thin skin on top. Add the dry espresso or coffee and whisk to dissolve. Add the chocolate and stir occasionally over heat for 1 minute. Remove the pan from the heat and whisk until the chocolate is all melted and the mixture is smooth. Let the icing stand at room temperature, stirring occasionally, for about 15 minutes until it barely begins to thicken.

Then stir it to mix and pour it slowly over the top of the cake, pouring it onto the middle. Use a long, narrow metal spatula to smooth the top and spread the icing so that a little of it runs down the sides (not too much--the icing on the sides should be a much thinner layer than on the top). With a small, narrow metal spatula, smooth the sides. Remove the strips of paper by pulling each one out toward a narrow end.

Baking with Yeast Doughs, 1/23/08

- *Oliebollen*, Dutch New Year's Fritters
- Cinnamon Rolls
- Hot Sticky Buns

Dutch New Year's Fritters, *Oliebollen*

- 1 package dry yeast
- 1 cup lukewarm milk (105-115°F)
- 2 ¼ cups all-purpose flour
- 2 tsp salt
- 1 egg
- 1 ½ cup raisins
- 1 Granny Smith apple - peeled, cored and finely chopped
- 1 quart vegetable oil for deep-frying
- 1 cup confectioners' sugar for dusting

Stir yeast into the warm milk. Let stand for a few minutes or until bubbling. Combine the flour and salt into a large bowl. Stir the yeast mixture and egg into the flour and mix into a smooth batter. Stir in the raisins and apples.

Cover the bowl, and leave the batter in a warm place to rise until double in size. This will take about 1 hour.

Heat the oil in a deep-fryer, or heavy deep pan to 375°F.

Use two spoons to shape scoops of dough into balls, and drop carefully into the hot oil. Fry the balls until golden brown, about 8 minutes. The doughnuts should be soft and not greasy. If the oil is not hot enough, the outside will be tough and the insides greasy. Drain finished doughnuts on paper towels and dust with confectioners' sugar.

Serve piled on a dish with more confectioners' sugar dusted over them. Eat as hot as possible.

Makes 12-16.

Cinnamon Rolls

- 1 ¼ cup mashed potatoes
- 1 cup milk
- ½ cup plus 1 tbsp sugar
- ½ tsp salt
- 2 tbsp unsalted butter, cut up
- ¼ cup warm water (105-115°F)
- 1 package dry yeast
- 1 egg
- 1 tsp vanilla extract
- 4 ¼ cups all purpose flour

Heat mashed potatoes, milk, ½ cup sugar, salt and butter in a saucepan over low heat until it reaches 105-115°F. Set aside.

Combine warm water with remaining 1 tbsp sugar and yeast and set aside until bubbling and frothy. In a small bowl beat egg and vanilla. In a large bowl, combine potato mixture, yeast mixture and egg. Gradually add in flour.

Knead dough for about 5 minutes, using more flour if necessary. Place dough in a greased bowl and cover with plastic wrap. Let rise in a warm place until doubled in size (1½ hrs.) When dough has risen, punch down and roll into 18" square.

Cinnamon Roll Filling
- 1/3 cup brown sugar
- 2 tsp cinnamon
- 2 tbsp melted butter
- 1 cup raisins

Preheat oven to 375°F. Combine sugar, cinnamon and raisins. Brush melted butter on rolled out dough, sprinkle sugar mixture on top. Roll up dough like a jelly roll, and cut into 12 equal pieces. Place in greased 9X13 inch pan (4 rows, 3 buns in each.) Cover loosely and allow to rise another hour, until doubled. Bake for about 20 minutes, until nicely browned. Remove from oven, let stand about 5 minutes, and then glaze.

Cinnamon Roll Glaze
- 1 cup confectioners' sugar
- 1 tsp vanilla
- 2 tbsp cream

Mix ingredients -- it should be quite thick, adjusting sugar or cream as needed. Drizzle over buns, and let stand until cool.

Hot Sticky Buns

- ½ cup warm water
- 2 tbsp granulated sugar
- 1 envelope yeast
- 1 cup milk
- 4 cups flour
- ½ tsp salt
- 1 egg yolk

Stir together water, sugar and yeast. Set aside until bubbling and foamy. Heat milk to 105-115°F. In a large bowl, combine the milk with 3 cups flour, yeast mixture, egg yolk and salt.

Turn out the dough and add enough of the remaining flour as necessary to handle the dough. Knead the dough until smooth and springy, about 5 minutes. Place dough in greased bowl, cover with plastic wrap and let rise until doubled about 1 hour. While dough is rising, prepare

Sticky Bun Topping:
- 1 cup brown sugar
- ½ cup honey
- 1 cup butter
- 1 ½ cups pecan halves

In a saucepan over low heat, combine butter, sugar and honey. Boil until sugar is dissolved, remove from heat and add pecans. Grease a 12 cup non-stick muffin pan well and distribute topping evenly between the cups.

Sticky Bun Filling:
- ¼ cup granulated sugar
- ¼ cup brown sugar
- 2 tsp cinnamon
- 1 cup chopped pecans
- 2 ounces melted butter

Once the dough has risen, punch down dough and roll out into large rectangle. Brush dough with melted butter, and sprinkle with filling. Roll dough up like a jelly roll. Cut into 12 equal pieces and place, cut side up in muffin cups, on top of the topping. Let rise until double, about 1 hour. While it is rising, preheat oven to 350°F. Place a large cookie sheet under the muffin pan, to catch any topping that may boil out. Bake for 25-30 minutes. After removing from oven, place a cookie sheet on top of pan and invert. Serve immediately.

Desserts with Vanessa, 2/27/09

- **Churros with Chocolate Sauce**
- **Boulders Inn Lemon Pie**
- **Classic Crème Brûlée**

Aunt Fannie, who used to live here at 160 Main Street, really enjoyed this class.

Boulders Inn Lemon Pie

- 4 egg whites (separate and reserve yolks for filling below)
- 1 cup granulated sugar
- ¼ tsp cream of tartar

Vanessa's parents, Kees and Ulla Adema, owned the Boulders Inn in New Preston, CT for many years. This was a huge favorite with the guests.

Meringue Crust: Beat the egg whites with cream of tartar until they start to thicken. Slowly add the sugar until the meringue is formed. Spoon into a well-greased pie tin. Let dry out in a 200F oven for 2 ½ to 3 hours.

- 4 egg yolks(from above)
- ½ cup sugar
- grated rind of 1 lemon
- 1/3 cup lemon juice
- 1/3 cup heavy cream

Lemon Filling: Beat the yolks with the sugar until pale and thick. Add lemon rind and juice and mix well. Cook over double boiler until thick and 160º F. Pour into a dish and refrigerate.

To assemble, whip the cream and fold into the lemon custard. Spread filling into meringue crust and serve.

Classic Crème Brûlée

- 2 extra-large egg plus 3 extra-large egg yolks
- ½ cup sugar, plus 1 tbsp for each serving
- 3 cups heavy cream
- 1 tbsp pure vanilla extract
- 1 tbsp orange liqueur (like Grand Marnier)

Preheat oven to 300°F. In the bowl of an electric mixer fitted with the paddle attachment, mix the egg, egg yolks, and ½ cup of the sugar together on low speed until just combined.

Meanwhile, scald the cream in a small saucepan until it is very hot to the touch but not boiled. With the mixer on low speed, slowly add the cream to the eggs. Add the vanilla and orange liqueur and pour into 5 or 6 8-ounce ramekins until almost full.

Place the ramekins in a baking pan and carefully pour boiling water into the pan to come halfway up the sides of the ramekins. Bake for 35-40 minutes, until the custards are set when gently shaken. Remove from the water bath, cool to room temperature, and refrigerate until firm.

To serve, spread 1 tbsp of sugar evenly on the top of each ramekin and heat with a kitchen blowtorch until the sugar caramelizes evenly. Allow to sit at room temperature for a minute until the caramelized sugar hardens.

Makes 5-6 servings.

Churros with Chocolate Sauce

- 8 tbsp unsalted butter
- 1 ½ cup whole milk
- 1 tsp kosher salt
- 1 tbsp cinnamon

- 1 cup sugar
- 1 ½ cup flour
- 3 large eggs, lightly beaten
- 2 quarts peanut oil

In a shallow pan, combine the cinnamon and sugar; set aside. In a small saucepan, melt the butter with the milk and salt over medium heat and bring to a boil. Add the flour and cook, stirring constantly, until a dough forms and pulls away from the sides of the pan, about 30 seconds. Remove from the heat and cool for 3 minutes. Stir the eggs into the batter until smooth. Fill a pastry bag fitted with a large star tip with batter.

In a medium pot, heat about 3 inches of oil to 350 °. Hold the pastry bag several inches above the oil, squeeze out the batter and snip it with kitchen shears when it reaches 4 inches long. Fry in batches, turning once, until deep golden brown, about 4 minutes. Using a slotted spoon, transfer to a paper-towel-lined plate to drain. While still hot, roll in the cinnamon sugar. Can be made ahead and kept warm in low-temperature oven. Serve with chocolate sauce. Makes about 20.

- 6-8 cups whole milk
- 2 large bars semisweet chocolate , chopped

- 3 tbsp butter
- 3 tbsp sugar
- orange or lemon zest (optional)

Authentic Spanish Chocolate Sauce: In a medium saucepan, heat the milk until small bubbles form around the edge, add the chocolate, butter and sugar, and zest, if desired, and cook for 30-40 minutes, stirring frequently, or until sauce becomes thick and pudding-like. Serve hot.

Dinner Classes

Lebanese Meza Cooking Class, 1/27/09

- Eggplant Salad, *Baba Ghanouj*
- Hummus
- Fried Cauliflower
- Parsley-Tahini Dip
- *Man'oosh*, Thyme Flatbread
- *Lahm b'Ajeen*, Lamb Flatbread
- Cabbage Slaw
- Garlic Sauce
- Garlic Chicken Wings

Eggplant Salad, *Baba Ghanouj*

- 3-4 medium eggplants, sliced lengthwise or 1 large eggplant
- ½ cup sesame tahini
- 1 tsp salt
- ½ tsp white pepper
- ½ cup extra-virgin olive oil
- juice of 1-2 lemons, to taste
- 4 cloves garlic, crushed
- pomegranate seeds and chopped parsley for garnish

This is a (safer) variation on the typical Lebanese method of placing a huge eggplant on an open burner and charring it.

Brush the sliced sides of the eggplants with olive oil and place them on a cookie sheet, skin sides facing up. Put the eggplants in the oven and broil the outer skins until charred. If the skins burn a little, don't worry, it is part of what makes this dish taste so good!

Remove eggplants from the oven and let them cool. In the meantime, juice the lemons. Once the eggplants are cool (it may take a little while), scoop the cooked insides into a large bowl. Add the garlic, white pepper and salt and stir together. Then add, alternating, the lemon juice and the tahini until the mixture becomes smooth. It should be a little thick, so going easy on the lemon juice is best.

When the baba ghanouj is the right taste and consistency for you, make a moat in the mixture and fill with olive oil, sprinkle with pomegranate seeds and parsley, and serve with hot pita.

Hummus

- 4 cups cooked chick peas (if canned, rinse before using)
- 1 scant cup sesame tahini
- 1 tsp salt
- 4 lemons, juiced
- 6 garlic cloves, crushed
- ¼ cup extra-virgin olive oil
- a dash of sweet paprika
- 1 tbsp toasted pine nuts

Several hours (or the night) before soak chick peas in 3 times their volume of water with the baking soda (optional, the latter will soften them and reduce cooking time.) The chick peas should double in size.

Rinse the soaked chick peas under cold water. Place in a saucepan, cover well with cold water, and place over a high heat. Bring to a boil. Reduce heat, cover and cook for about 1 ½ hours or until very tender. Drain, reserving some of the cooking water. Also, reserve a few whole chick peas for garnish.

In a food processor or blender, blend chick peas to a smooth puree add tahini, salt to taste and blend well together. Pour in half the lemon juice gradually, and taste. Add garlic and mix again. If it is too thick add some of the reserved cooking water to thin; the puree should be soft and creamy but not runny.

Pour into small shallow bowls, make a dip in the center and add a few whole chick peas or pine nuts (either raw or toasted) in the center then pour olive oil over them. Sprinkle paprika around edges of bowl.

Tahini-Parsley Dip

- ½ cup + 2 tbsp sesame tahini
- 1-2 lemons, juiced
- 7 tbsp water

- 2 oz chopped parsley
- 2 cloves garlic, crushed
- salt to taste

Put tahini in a mixing bowl and add the water and lemon juice alternately, always turning spoon in same direction. Whether this is tradition or superstition, we're not sure, but it does work. The mixture will first thicken, then get thinner. Continue until you get the consistency of labneh (greek yoghurt.) Stir in the garlic, parsley, add salt to taste and mix well.

Fried Cauliflower, *Arnabeet Miqli*

- 2 small cauliflowers, cut into medium-sized florets
- salt to taste

- vegetable oil for frying
- pomegranate molasses (*Ribb al-Rumman*)

Blanch the florets for 2-3 minutes, or until half-cooked, then drain and dry on paper towels.

Heat enough oil in a skillet or pot to deep fry the cauliflower. Oil should be hot enough that when you test with a floret the oil should bubble around it. Fry (in batches if necessary) until golden all over. Remove with slotted spoon and drain on paper towels.

Serve at room temperature with a side dish of yoghurt or with a drizzle of Pomegranate Molasses (a great Lebanese favorite of ours, now available in most specialty and organic food stores.)

Thyme Flatbread, *Man'oosh*

- 2 ¼ tsp active dry yeast
- 2 cups   all-purpose flour
- ¾ cup warm water (105-115°F)
- 1½ tsp salt
- 1½ tsp olive oil for dough plus 8 tbsp for topping
- 3 oz Lebanese zaatar spice (a mix of dried thyme, sumac and sesame seeds)

The dough can be made a day in advance – let it rise slowly, covered, in the refrigerator. Bring to room temperature before using.

Stir together yeast, 1 tbsp flour, and ¼ cup warm water in a measuring cup and let stand until mixture develops creamy foam on surface, about 5 minutes. (If mixture doesn't foam, discard and start over with new yeast.)

Stir together 1 ¼ cups flour with salt in a large bowl. Add yeast mixture, oil, and remaining ½ cup warm water and stir until smooth. Stir in enough flour (about 1/2 cup) to make dough come away from sides of bowl. Knead dough on lightly floured surface with lightly floured hands until smooth, soft, and elastic, about 8 minutes. Form dough into a ball, put on a lightly floured surface, and generously dust with flour. Loosely cover with plastic wrap and let rise in a warm draft-free place until doubled in bulk, about 1¼ hours. Do not punch down dough.

Preheat oven to 450°F. Carefully dredge dough in a bowl of flour to coat and transfer to a dry work surface. Make 3-4 inch rounds by pinching off a handful of dough and rolling.

Combine the remaining olive oil with the zaatar stirring well to make a smooth paste. Spread thinly on each pizza you form.

Bake for 10 minutes or until cooked through. Serve with tomatoes and cucumbers to make a delicious hot "wrap"!

Makes 4 large or 12 small flatbreads.

Lamb Flatbreads, *Lahm b'Aajeen*

- 1 onion, finely chopped
- 1 ½ tomatoes, diced
- 9 oz lean lamb, ground
- 1 tsp lemon juice

- ¼ tsp ground cinnamon
- ½ tsp ground allspice
- 2 tbsp pine nuts
- salt and pepper to taste

Combine onions and tomatoes in a mixing bowl, season with salt and pepper and mix firmly with hands. Squeeze to drain excess juices. Add meat and remaining ingredients, except pine nuts, and mix well with hands until well-blended. Let stand for 10-15 minutes. Spread a small amount on each pizza, to cover flatly and thinly. Sprinkle pine nuts on top. Bake in a preheated oven for 10-12 minutes or until bread and nuts are golden brown. Makes 4 large or 12 small flatbreads.

NB: You can always buy fresh pre-made dough from the supermarket or a pizza place, if you are in a hurry.

Cabbage Slaw, *Salatet Malfouf*

- 1 medium cabbage
- 2 garlic cloves, crushed
- 4 tbsp olive oil

- salt to taste
- black pepper to taste
- 1 lemon, juiced

Clean and quarter the cabbage, remove core, then shred finely. Combine dressing ingredients and mix well. Pour over salad and toss.

Let stand 10-15 minutes then mix well again before serving.

Garlic Wings, *Jawaneh b'Toum*

- 12 chicken wings
- 8 garlic cloves, crushed
- 2 tbsp olive oil
- 1 lemon, juiced
- ¼ tsp cinnamon
- ½ tsp ground allspice
- salt and pepper to taste
- pinch of cayenne pepper

Rinse the chicken wings in cold water and pat dry. Make marinade with remaining ingredients in a large bowl, add wings and coat well. Marinate in the refrigerator overnight, or at room temperature for at least 2 hours. Bake in a 400ºF oven for about 15 minutes on a side, until crispy and even a little dark. Serve with garlic sauce, below.

Serves 4-6.

Lebanese Garlic Dip for Chicken, *Toum*

- 8 garlic cloves
- ¼ tsp sea salt
- ½ lemon, juiced
- 4 tbsp olive oil
- 1 small potato, mashed

Typically served on the side with roasted chicken, it is also a perfect accompaniment to these chicken wings.

Place garlic and salt in a mortar and pound to a paste. Place in a mixing bowl and lemon juice, then slowly whisk in olive oil until creamy. To adjust "garlicky" taste and extend, mix in the mashed potato, and whisk until you get a smooth, creamy consistency.

Spa Cooking inspired by Martha Stewart & Canyon Ranch, 1/15/09

- **Shiitake & Bok Choi Noodle Soup**
- **Marinated Cucumber Salad**
- **Fish in Parchment with Bok Choi**
- **Jasmine Rice, Shiitakes and Scallions**
- **Vanilla-Ginger Asian Pears**

Shiitake & Bok Choi Noodle Soup

- 1 lb baby bok choi
- ½ pound fresh shiitake mushrooms
- 8 scallions chopped
- 8 grams katsuobushi (dried bonito flakes; about 2/3 cup)
- 6 ounces thin Asian buckwheat noodles

Cut bok choi crosswise into ¼-inch-thick slices. Discard stems from mushrooms and cut caps into thin slices. Cut scallions into thin slices.

In a 6-quart pot, bring 6 cups water to a boil with the bonito flakes and boil 1 minute. Pour stock through a fine sieve into a large bowl and discard bonito flakes.

Return stock to pot and add bok choi, mushrooms, and noodles. Simmer soup, uncovered, until noodles are tender, 2 to 5 minutes, depending on type of noodle.

Season with salt and pepper and stir in scallions. Serves 4 as a main course, 6-8 as appetizer

Marinated Asian Cucumber Salad

- 2 English cucumbers
- 1/3 cup rice wine vinegar
- 1/3 cup soy sauce
- 1/3 cup vegetable Oil

Slice cucumbers into thin rounds using a sharp knife or mandolin. Mix dressing, adjust to taste, and toss cucumber rounds in, coating thoroughly, cover and chill for 15-20 minutes before serving.   Serves 6-8 as a side or salad.

Jasmine Rice with Shiitakes and Scallions

- 4 cups water
- 2 cups jasmine rice
- 6 tbsp extra-virgin olive oil
- coarse salt and black pepper
- 8 oz shiitake fresh mushrooms, stems discarded
- 6 garlic cloves, thinly-sliced
- 3 tbsp rice wine vinegar
- 3 scallions

Bring water and rice to a boil in a small pot. Reduce heat, cover and simmer until water is absorbed, about 15 minutes. Remove from heat, stir in one tbsp oil and season with salt and pepper. Cover and let stand.

Heat remaining oil in a large sauté pan over medium-high heat. Add shiitakes in a single layer and cook until brown and crisp about 3 minutes. Reduce heat to medium and cook for 2 minutes more. Add garlic and cook until light-gold in color, about 2 minutes. Stir in vinegar and season with salt and pepper. Transfer rice to a platter, top with shiitake mixture. Thinly cut scallions and sprinkle on top before serving.

Serves 8.

Halibut & Baby Bok Choi in Parchment

- 4 limes zested and juiced
- juice of 2 lemons
- 4 pieces of fresh ginger, peeled and julienned
- 2 red onions, halved and sliced very thinly
- 8 garlic cloves, sliced thinly
- 8 fish fillets, 6-8 oz each
- 8 heads baby bok choi, quartered lengthwise
- 1 cup extra-virgin olive oil
- salt and black pepper
- 1 bunch fresh cilantro

Preheat oven to 450°F.

Mix lime zest, juices, garlic slices, ginger and onions in a medium bowl.

Fold eight 16x24" pieces of parchment in half lengthwise. Unfold, and place 1 halibut fillet and 1 head of bok choi along each crease. Rub both generously with olive oil and season with salt and pepper. Top each fillet with some onion mixture and 2-3 sprigs of cilantro.

Fold parchment over fish, making small overlapping folds along edges and sealing with a paper clip. Place on a rimmed baking sheet. Roast until parchment puffs, about 10-12 minutes.

Be sure to cut packets open carefully to avoid escaping steam.

Serves 8.

Vanilla-Ginger Asian Pears

- 4 medium Asian Pears (Nashi/star apple) cored
- 4" piece of ginger peeled and thinly sliced

- 2 vanilla beans, split and scraped, pod reserved
- 1 ½ cups sugar
- 6 cups of water

Cut each pear in quarters lengthwise, then slice each quarter in half, then place in a large bowl.

Bring ginger, vanilla seeds and pod, sugar and water to a boil in a small saucepan for 3 minutes. Pour mixture over pears. Cover tightly with plastic wrap and refrigerate until cold, about 1 hour.

Discard vanilla pods and ginger. Divide the pears in 8 bowls and serve. And if you leave it to chill overnight, the flavors really develop.

Serves 8

Provençal Dinner Class, 1/24/09

- **Herb-Leaf Salad**
- **Braised Chicken Provençal-style**
- **Chick-pea and Green Lentil Salad with Sun-dried Tomato Vinaigrette**
- **Pistachio and Strawberry Floating Island**

Five Herb Leaf Salad

- 1 tsp sherry wine vinegar
- 1 tsp red wine vinegar
- Juice of ½ a lemon
- salt and pepper to taste
- 2 ½ tbsp extra-virgin olive oil
- 1 bunch parsley rinsed, dried, and stemmed
- 1 bunch chives, rinsed, dried, and minced
- 1 bunch dill, rinsed, dried, stemmed, and chopped
- 1 bunch tarragon, rinsed, dried and stemmed,
- 1 bunch mint, rinsed and stemmed,

In a large, shallow salad bowl, whisk together the vinegars, lemon juice and salt. Whisk in the oil and pepper. Taste for seasoning and add salt and pepper.

Add all the herb leaves and toss to evenly coat the greens with the dressing. Taste for seasoning again.

Serves 4-6 in small portions as an accompaniment.

Chick-pea and Green Lentil Salad

- 4 cups water
- 1 cup green lentils, picked through, rinsed
- 2 cups cooked chickpeas
- 1 red onion, halved, peeled, diced fine
- salt and pepper to taste
- 1 red bell pepper, diced fine
- 1 cucumber, peeled, halved, seeded, and diced fine
- 8 marinated sun-dried tomatoes, julienned
- 2/3 cup fresh basil leaves, sliced

Place water and lentils in a big saucepan, and bring to a boil over high heat. Lower heat and simmer uncovered 20-25 minutes, until the lentils are tender. Drain the lentils and place in a large bowl. Drain and rinse the canned or soaked chickpeas, then add to the lentils. Add the remaining ingredients except the basil. Now make the vinaigrette.

Sun-dried Tomato Vinaigrette

- 15 marinated sun-dried tomatoes
- 2 garlic cloves, minced
- ½ cup balsamic vinegar
- salt and pepper to taste
- 2/3 cup grated Parmesan cheese
- 1/3 cup olive oil

Put everything except the olive oil into the bowl of a food processor fitted with a metal blade, and purée to a thick paste. Add the oil slowly through the feed tube until consistency is smooth. Taste and adjust for salt.

Add to the beans and toss until they are evenly coated with the vinaigrette. Sprinkle the basil over the salad and toss again, gently. Taste for salt. Cover and refrigerate for at least an hour, so the beans can absorb the flavor of the vinaigrette. Garnish with more basil if desired.

Serves 6.

Chicken Provençal-style

- 4-5 medium tomatoes cut into wedges
- 1 large onion, cut into wedges, leaving root ends intact
- 2/3 cup drained brine-cured black olives, pitted
- 6 large garlic cloves, sliced, plus 1 tsp minced
- 4 tbsp olive oil, divided
- 2 tsp salt and 1 tsp pepper
- 2 tsp herbes de Provence, (usu. rosemary, marjoram, basil, bay leaf, thyme, and sometimes lavender flowers, the proportions vary)
- ½ tsp fennel seeds
- 1 small chicken cut into small parts
- parsley for garnish

Preheat oven to 400°F with rack in middle. Toss together tomatoes, onion, olives, sliced garlic, 3 tbsp oil, half the herbes de Provence, fennel seeds, and half of the salt and pepper in a shallow baking dish.

Stir together minced garlic, remaining salt and pepper and herbes de Provence, and remaining tablespoon olive oil.

Remove excess fat from chicken and pat dry, then rub with seasoning mixture. Place in pan with the vegetables. Roast until an instant-read thermometer inserted into thickest part of a thigh (do not touch bone) registers 170°F, about 1 hour in convection oven, 1 ¼ hours in regular oven.

Let the chicken stand 10 minutes before serving with vegetables and pan juices. Garnish with chopped parsley and serve accompanied with hot bread.

Serves 4.

Pistachio and Strawberry Floating Island

- 1 tsp unsalted butter
- 4 large egg whites
- ½ cup granulated sugar
- ¾ cup coarsely chopped shelled pistachios
- 4 large strawberries, hulled and cut into ¼ inch dice
- 10 oz strawberries, hulled
- 1 cup black currant preserves with whole berries
- 3 tbsp créme de cassis
- 3 tbsp toasted almonds
- extra smaller (ripe-red) strawberries for garnish

Based on Jacques Pépin's variation on the classic French Ile Flottante, this wonderful dessert is impressive, yet easy to make.

Preheat oven to 350 F. Grease a 6 cup loaf pan with the butter. Beat the egg whites until stiff. Add the sugar all at once, and beat for a few seconds. Fold the pistachios and the diced berries into the beaten whites, and transfer the mixture to the loaf pan.

Place the pan in a larger vessel, and surround it with warm tap water. Bake at 350°F for 30 minutes, and then remove the pan from the water bath and allow to cool on a rack. The dessert will deflate slightly. The recipe can be prepared to this point up to 1 day ahead, covered with plastic wrap, and refrigerated.

Slice two or three strawberries to use for garnish, and set them aside. Place the remaining strawberries and preserves in the bowl of a food processor and process until pureed. Add the créme de cassis.

To serve, unmold on a rectangular platter. Sprinkle with a little sauce, and decorate with the sliced berries and toasted almonds. Divide the remaining sauce among six dessert plates, and top with a slice of the cold floating island. 6 servings.

Moroccan Dinner, 2/21/07

- Chickpeas with Turmeric
- Couscous
- Harissa
- Preserved Lemons
- Tagine
- Briwat

This was one of our all-time favorite classes!

We had so much fun learning and adapting these recipes from Paula Wolfert's and Claudia Roden's excellent cookbooks, and even more fun sharing them.

The short-cut method for preserved lemons works marvelously.

Chickpeas with Turmeric

In Morocco, this is considered poor people's food. A grander version uses ½ tsp of saffron threads instead of the turmeric. Note that if you use canned chickpeas, the cooking time is reduced to just 10-15 minutes.

- 2 ½ cups water
- 4 tbsp olive oil
- 1 large onion, chopped
- 5 garlic cloves, crushed
- ½ tsp ground turmeric
- salt and pepper

- 1 ½ cups dried chickpeas soaked overnight in plenty of cold water and drained
- 4 tbsp chopped cilantro
- 3 tbsp chopped parsley

Heat the oil in a large pan and fry the onion until lightly colored. Add the garlic and stir for a moment or two. Stir in turmeric, and then add in the drained chickpeas.

Cover with 2 ½ cups water and simmer for 1 ½ hours or until chickpeas are very tender, adding salt and pepper to taste when they have softened, and extra water if it becomes too dry. The liquid should be reduced to a thick sauce at the end.

Stir in the chopped parsley and cilantro and cook for 5 minutes more before serving hot with bread to sop up sauce.

Serves 4.

Couscous

Here is Paula Wolfert's foolproof method of preparing precooked couscous. You need the same volume of salted water as couscous, and need to allow about 1 lb for 4 people.

Put 2 ½ cups couscous in an oven dish. Gradually add 2 ½ cups warm salted water (made with about ¾ tsp salt,) stirring vigorously so that water is absorbed evenly. Leave to swell for 10 minutes.

Mix in 2 tbsp excellent extra-virgin olive oil, and rub the couscous between your hands to air it and break up any lumps.

Put the dish in an oven preheated to 400°F and heat through for 20 minutes or until it is steaming hot.

Before serving, work in 3 tbsp butter cut into small pieces (or 3 tbsp of very good olive oil) breaking any lumps and let it fluff up again before serving.

Harissa Sauce

- 1 oz dried red chili peppers
- 2 cloves garlic
- 2 tsp ground caraway
- salt to taste
- extra-virgin olive oil
- mortar and pestle

Cover peppers with hot water and soak for an hour. Drain and cut into small pieces. Place in mortar and pound into a puree with the garlic and spices. Sprinkle with a little salt.

To preserve, spoon into a jar with a tight-fitting lid, cover with a layer of olive oil. Seal tightly and refrigerate.

Orange and Grated Carrot Salad

- 1 lb carrots
- 1 navel orange
- 1 tsp cinnamon
- 3 tbsp lemon juice
- 1 tbsp granulated sugar
- 1 tsp orange blossom water
- pinch of salt

Clean, peel and grate the carrots. Peel and section the orange, and reserve the juice. Mix the juice with the remaining ingredients. Stir in the carrots and orange segments, and then chill for at least 1 hour.

Before serving, drain partially if there is too much liquid.

Serves 4 as a salad or side.

Preserved Lemons

These lemons, boiled in brine and preserved in oil, give excellent results in a few days instead of the usual weeks it takes. This method from Claudia Roden is unorthodox but gives excellent results.

With a sharp knife, make 8 superficial (till you just see the white) incisions into the skin of each of 4 lemons, from one end to the other. Place the lemons in a large pan with salted water using 4 tbsp salt for 4 lemons. Put a smaller lid on top of the lemons to weight them down so they do not float, and boil them for 25 minutes or until the peel is very soft.

Drain the water and set aside. When cool lemons are enough to handle, scoop out the flesh, pack the skins in a glass jar and cover with a light vegetable or sunflower oil.

By the 3rd or 4th day, the lemon skins will be a perfect replacement for the traditional preserved lemons which you can buy in a jar in Morocco.

Chicken Tagine with Olives & Lemons

- 4 tbsp olive oil
- 2 onions, grated
- 4 garlic cloves, crushed
- ½ tsp crushed saffron threads
- 1 tsp ground ginger
- 1 chicken cut into 8 pieces
- salt and black pepper
- juice of ½ lemon
- 2 tbsp chopped coriander
- 2 tbsp chopped parsley
- peel of 3 preserved lemons
- 24 green olives

In a wide oven-proof casserole, heat the oil and put in the onions. Sauté, stirring, over low heat until onions soften, then stir in the garlic, saffron and ginger.

Season the chicken pieces with salt and pepper, and put in pot. Simmer, covered, and turn the pieces over a few times (add water if they become too dry.)   After about 25 minutes, lift out the breasts and set aside. Continue to cook the remaining pieces for about 15 minutes, and then return the breasts to the pan.

Stir in the lemon juice, coriander, parsley, lemon peel (cut into quarters or strips) and the olives. Simmer, uncovered for 5-10 minutes, until the reduced sauce is thick and unctuous. (If there is too much liquid, remove the chicken pieces, reduce and then return them to the pan.)

Serve each piece with 3 or 4 olives and a slice or two of lemon peel, and drizzle sauce over.

Serves 8.

Rolled Almond Pastries in Syrup, *Briwat b'Loz*

- ½ lb clear honey
- ½ cup water
- ½ cup ground almonds
- ½ cup superfine sugar
- 1 tsp ground cinnamon
- 3 tbsp orange blossom water
- 14 sheets of fillo dough
- 5 tbsp unsalted butter, melted

Bring honey and water to a boil and let simmer for half a minute. Cool.

Mix the ground almonds with sugar, cinnamon and orange blossom water.

Only when you are ready to make the pastries, open the package of fillo dough and brush the top one with melted butter.

Place a line of about 2 tbsp of the almond mixture at one of the short ends of a fillo rectangle, into a line about ¾" from the short and long edges. Roll up loosely into a fat cigar shape. Turn the ends in about a third of the way along to trap the filling, and then continue to roll the ends opened out.

Repeat with the remaining 13 sheets of fillo.

Place finished pastries on a baking sheet and brush lightly with the remaining butter, and bake in an oven preheated to 300°F for 30 minutes or until lightly golden and crisp.

Remove from oven. While still warm and crisp, turn each pastry quickly in the syrup. Arrange on a dish and let cool. When cold, serve with the remaining syrup poured over.

An Elegant Indian Dinner, 1/25/08

- **Pappadoms**
- **Chapati** (see recipe page 56)
- **Khatte Cholé**   (see recipe page 27)
- **Chicken Murgh Khorma**
- **Goan-style Shrimp Curry**
- **Coconut Rice Pudding**

Pappadoms, a thin peppery wafer, and an important part of Sindhi and Gujarati cuisine. You can purchase them in health food, specialty or ethnic shops.

The curry leaves for the Goan Curry are amazing – and it is worth the effort to go to an Indian food store to find them.

Chicken in Yoghurt-Almond Sauce, *Murgh Khorma*

- 3" piece of fresh ginger, peeled and chopped
- 6 cloves garlic, peeled and chopped
- 4 tbsp blanched slivered almonds
- 1 ½ cups plain yogurt
- ½ tsp garam masala spices
- 1 tbsp ground coriander
- ½ tsp cayenne pepper
- 1 ½ tsp salt
- 5 tbsp peanut or olive oil
- 2 onions, peeled, cut in half lengthwise, then cut into fine half-rings
- two 3" sticks cinnamon
- 8 whole cardamom pods
- 2 bay leaves
- 1 chicken cut in 8 pieces
- 3 tbsp golden raisins
- 3 tbsp finely chopped fresh cilantro for garnish

Cut the chicken up for a curry: remove all skin, halve each breast piece and separate legs from thighs. Reserve remaining chicken for another use, e.g. stock. Put the ginger, garlic and ¼ cup water in a blender, and blend to a smooth paste. Add almonds and 2 tbsp water, and blend to a smooth paste again. Put the yogurt in a bowl, and whisk lightly until smooth. Add the garam masala, ground coriander, cayenne and salt, and stir well to mix.

Heat the oil in your largest frying pan, preferably non-stick, and add onion slices, stir and fry for 10-12 minutes, lowering heat if necessary, until onion is reddish brown. Remove with a slotted spoon, squeezing to drain as much oil as possible back into the pan. Spread onion-slices on paper towels. Add cinnamon, cardamom, and bay leaves, and lower heat to medium. Stir once or twice, then working in batches of 2 or 3 pieces at a time, lightly brown the chicken on both sides and set aside as done. Add golden raisins to pan, stir a few times, then add paste from the blender. Stir and fry for 2 minutes.

Now add all the ingredients into the pan, stirring to mix, and bring to a simmer. Cover, turn heat to low, and cook gently 25-30 minutes, stirring gently now and then, till chicken is tender. Garnish and serve. Serves 6-8.

Goan-style Shrimp Curry

- 1 lb large or extra-large shrimp, peeled and deveined

Marinade:
- ½ tsp kosher salt
- ½ tsp ground peppercorns
- ¼ tsp cayenne pepper
- 3 tbsp lemon juice

Sauce:
- 1 cup water
- ¼ cup canola oil
- 24 curry leaves, roughly torn
- 4 dried red chilies
- 1 tsp ground peppercorns
- 4" piece of ginger, minced
- 1 red onion, finely chopped
- 1 ½ tbsp kosher salt
- 3 garlic cloves, peeled and chopped
- 2 tsp ground coriander
- ½ tsp ground turmeric
- 2 cups canned chopped tomatoes
- ½ tsp curry powder
- 1 ½ cups coconut milk
- 1 cup chopped fresh cilantro

Add all marinade ingredients in a gallon-size zip lock bag, add shrimp and toss thoroughly to coat. Seal bag and refrigerate.

Set ½ cup of water next to the stovetop. Heat the oil with the curry leaves and chilies in a medium pot over high heat, until leaves start to sizzle, 1-2 minutes. Add ground peppercorns, and cook 1 minute longer. Stir in ginger, onion and salt, and cook, stirring often, until onion is browned, about 8 minutes, sprinkling with water and stirring whenever the onion and ginger begin to stick to bottom of pot.

Add garlic, coriander and turmeric, and cook until garlic is fragrant, about 1 minute. Reduce heat to medium-low and tomatoes to the pot. Cook, stirring and scraping the browned bits up from the sides and bottom o the pot, for 1 minute more. Increase heat to medium-high and simmer for 5 minutes, stirring often. Stir in the curry powder and cook for 1 minute and then pour in the coconut milk and ½ cup water. Bring to a boil and add the shrimp and accumulated juices from the bag.

Bring to a simmer and cook until shrimp are curled and opaque, about 2 minutes. Stir in chopped cilantro and serve.

Fresh, Local and Organic, 2/15/08

- Fresh Garlic Soup
- Boudin Blanc with Honey Crisp apples and Applejack
- Sauté of Chicken
- Mizuna and Mustard Greens with Dijon Vinaigrette
- Painted Goat Farms Chevre
- Vanessa's Huguenot Apple Torte

Fresh Local Garlic Soup

- 3 heads garlic
- 4 cups water
- 2 onions, finely chopped
- 2/3 cup extra-virgin olive oil
- 3 ½ cups chicken stock
- 10 fresh sage leaves
- four 1/2-inch-thick slices good-quality crusty bread
- 2/3 cup shredded Italian Parmesan cheese
- salt and black pepper to taste

Separate cloves from each head of garlic but do not peel. Bring water to a rolling boil in a 2-quart saucepan. Drop in garlic cloves and boil 10 minutes. Drain in a sieve and peel. Return the garlic cloves to the saucepan, and add the onion, olive oil, sage, and stock. Bring to a lively bubble over medium-high heat. Partially cover and cook 5 minutes. Uncover, adjust the heat so the liquid bubbles slowly, and cook another 5 minutes.

Croutons: Preheat broiler. While the soup is simmering, arrange the bread slices on a baking sheet. Toast under the broiler 1-2 minutes per side, or until the slices are crisp and golden. Set aside a few spoonfuls of the cheese to top the soup. Sprinkle the rest over the bread slices. Slip the baking sheet back under the broiler only a second or two, to melt the cheese but not brown it.

Finishing and Serving: Warm four soup dishes. The garlic cloves will be meltingly soft when the soup finishes cooking. Remove all but 1 sage leaf, and puree the soup in a blender or food processor. Season to taste. Arrange the croutons in the soup dishes, and pour the puree over them. Sprinkle each serving with a few shreds of cheese, and serve immediately.

Serves 4.

Boudin Blanc with Honey Crisp Apples and Applejack

- 1 lb boudin blanc
- 3 honey crisp apples, peeled, in thin wedges
- 3 tbsp butter
- 1 tbsp honey
- 1 tbsp chopped fresh thyme
- 3 tbsp applejack or Calvados

Poach, chill and then slice sausages on a slant into slices about ¾" thick. Melt 2 tbsp butter in a 9" skillet. Add apples and sauté till they begin to brown. Add honey and thyme and when the apples turn golden, add the applejack.

Allow the applejack to flame (or not) and cook for 1-2 minutes more and then remove from the heat.

In a second 9" skillet, melt 1 tbsp butter and when hot add the sliced sausage and brown thoroughly. Add the browned sausages to the apples, mix well and serve warm.

Chicken Sauté

- 4 lbs fresh chicken parts
- 4 tbsp unsalted butter
- 1 tbsp vegetable oil
- 1/3 cup dry white wine or dry white vermouth
- 1 cup chicken stock
- salt and black pepper
- 5 cloves unpeeled fresh garlic
- several sprigs fresh tarragon, thyme and sage (plus more for garnish)
- 3 tbsp minced shallots or scallions
- 1 tbsp unsalted butter
- fresh parsley for garnish

Set a pan or casserole over moderately high heat, swirl 2 tbsp of the butter and the oil all around the inside of it, and when the butter foam starts to subside lay in as many pieces of chicken as will fit comfortably in one layer without crowding. Turn the chicken every minute or so, letting all surfaces color a nice walnut brown. As each piece is ready, remove it to a clean tray and add another piece, until you have done them all. Pour out and discard all the browning fat, leaving the crusty browned bits in the pan. Pour the wine or vermouth into the pan and scrape into it these brown bits, adding a bit of the chicken stock if needed. Pour this liquid into the remaining stock and reserve for sauce.

Lightly season all of the chicken with salt and pepper. Set the pan over moderate heat, add the remaining butter, and when melted return the dark meat (drumsticks and thighs) to the pan. Cover and cook slowly 7-8 minutes. Then turn the dark meat over and add the white meat, which needs less cooking. Baste the chicken with accumulated pan juices, add the garlic, and then place the fresh herbs on top. Cover and continue cooking, turning the chicken several times for 15 minutes more. The chicken is done when the meat is tender if pressed.

Remove the chicken to a hot platter, cover, and keep warm for the few minutes it will take to make the sauce. Spoon out and discard excess fat from the pan juices, as well as the fresh herbs and the pieces of crushed garlic. Set the pan over medium heat, stir in the shallots or scallions, and boil rapidly for a minute. Then pour in the reserved wine and stock and boil over high heat, stirring any coagulated meat juice into the liquid with a wooden spoon. When reduced to a light syrup, remove from heat, swish with the optional butter, and spoon over the chicken.

Variation: Chicken Sauté with Potatoes, Lardons and Mushrooms

Follow the recipe above, with these additions.

- a little more oil and/or butter as needed
- lardons from a 5 oz slab of pancetta, bacon or salt pork
- 1 lb mushrooms, cleaned and quartered
- 4 medium-size boiling potatoes, peeled and quartered
- Salt and pepper to taste

Start browning the chicken. Now, heat a tsp of oil in a 10" frying pan and brown the lardons lightly. Remove with a slotted spoon and set aside, leaving their rendered fat in the pan. In it sauté the mushrooms, and set aside with the lardons. Drop the potatoes into a pan of lightly salted boiling water, bring again to the boil, and boil for 5 to 6 minutes, or until almost tender; drain, and reserve. Distribute lardons, mushrooms, and potatoes around and over the chicken as you start the final 20 minutes of cooking.

Northern Italian Dinner, 2/29/08

- **Creamed Mushrooms and Sage Toasts**
- **Fresh Asparagus Risotto**
- **Fennel, Orange and Olive Salad**
- **Homemade Pasta with Country Ragu**
- **Homemade Ricotta**
- **Torta di Ricotta al Dante**

Creamed Wild Mushrooms & Sage on Toast

- 1 ½ lbs wild mushrooms, oysters, chanterelles, morels, shiitakes or cremini
- 6 tbsp unsalted butter
- 3 garlic cloves, minced
- salt and pepper to taste
- 1 cup heavy cream
- 1/3 cup chicken stock
- 1 bunch fresh sage leaves
- 16-20 toasts

Trim and stem the mushrooms. Slice the tops in halves or quarters and in one skillet, melt half the butter then add the mushroom tops, season with salt and pepper and cook over moderately high heat, stirring, until golden.

Mince the stems and trimmings and in another skillet, fry the garlic and minced mushrooms in half the butter. In the meantime pick the sage leaves, reserving several whole ones for garnish. Chop the remaining sage leaves and add half to the mushrooms. Add the stock and reduce. Now add the cream and simmer over moderate heat until slightly thickened, about 5 minutes.

Combine both skillets, add the remaining chopped sage and simmer for 2-3 more minutes. Spoon onto toasts and serve.

Fennel, Orange and Olive Salad

- 2 bulbs fennel, cored and thinly sliced
- 4 large oranges
- 1 cup pitted black olives
- 1 red onion, thinly sliced
- 1/3 cup extra-virgin olive oil
- salt and pepper to taste

Slice the fennel bulbs into 4 quarters. Cut out and discard the piece of core in each quarter, and thinly slice the rest of the bulb. Peel the oranges over a large bowl. Peel or cut off all of the white membranes from the orange sections. (This is called making supremes.) Reserve any juice that gets squeezed out.

Combine the fennel, orange supremes, olives and onion in a large bowl. Add the olive oil and season with salt and pepper. Mix well, and allow to marinate for 1 to 2 hours for best flavor.

Serves 6 to 8

Classic Risotto

- 6 tbsp butter
- 3 tbsp finely chopped onions
- 2 cloves garlic finely chopped
- 2 cups arborio rice
- 1 tsp chopped stem saffron
- 5 cups chicken stock
- ½ cup dry white wine
- ¾ cup grated parmesan cheese
- salt and black pepper to taste

Heat 2 tbsp of the butter in a large casserole, then add onions and garlic and cook until wilted. Add rice, salt, pepper and saffron and stir to coat the grains. Separately, heat the stock and simmer.

Add wine to the rice and cook, stirring until all wine has evaporated. Add 1 cup of hot stock to the rice mixture, stirring gently until all liquid has been absorbed. Add another ½ cup of stock, and stirring, repeat as above.

Repeat, adding ½ cup every 3-4 minutes until all is absorbed. Fold in remaining butter and cheese.

Serves 4-6.

Basic Egg Pasta

- 3 ½ cups (14oz) all purpose unbleached flour or pasta flour (type 00)
- 4 large eggs, lightly beaten
- 1 tsp salt

Put flour and salt in a bowl or on a flat work surface. Stir to blend. Make a well in the center and add the eggs. With your fingertips gradually incorporate the flour into the eggs until you have a soft dough. (Depending on the weather and humidity, you may have to add a few tbsp of water; or alternatively some flour if the dough is very sticky.) Knead the dough on a floured work surface for 8-10 minutes until it is smooth and elastic. Cover with a napkin and allow to rest for at least 20-30 minutes.

When the dough is ready, cut into thirds or quarters. Work with one piece at a time and remember to keep the remaining pieces covered. Roll out on lightly floured surface, beginning from the center, to a thickness of about 1/8". Allow to dry for 15-20 minutes.

Sprinkle flour on the dough, then roll up dough and cut crosswise. Sizes: fettuccine: 0.3 cm (1/8"); tagliatelle: 0.5 cm (1/4"); pappardelle: 1 cm (1/2"). Makes about 1 lb dry pasta

Country-Style Meat Sauce, *Ragu alla Contadina*

- 3 tbsp extra-virgin olive oil
- 3 oz pancetta, chopped
- 1 onion, minced
- 2 stalks celery, minced
- 1 carrot, minced
- 6 oz veal
- 6 oz boneless pork loin
- 8 oz beef skirt steak
- 2 oz thin-sliced Prosciutto
- 1 cup dry red wine
- 1 ½ cups stock
- 2 cups milk
- 3 cans plum tomatoes
- salt and black pepper

Heat olive oil in a 12-inch skillet over medium-high heat. Add pancetta and minced vegetables and sauté, stirring frequently with a wooden spatula, 10 minutes, or until the onions barely begin to color. Coarsely grind all the meats together, including the prosciutto, in a food processor or meat grinder. Stir into the pan and slowly brown over medium heat.

The meats will give off liquid and turn dull gray, but as the liquid evaporates, browning will begin. Stir often, scooping under the meats with spatula. Protect the brown glaze forming on the bottom of the pan by turning the heat down. Cook 15 minutes, or until the meats are a deep brown. Turn the contents of the skillet into a strainer and shake out the fat. Turn them into the saucepan and set over medium heat.

Add the wine to the skillet, lowering the heat so the sauce bubbles quietly. Stir occasionally until the wine has reduced by half, about 3 minutes. Scrape up the brown glaze as the wine bubbles, then pour the reduced wine into the saucepan and set the skillet aside. If you are using stock, stir 1/2 cup into the saucepan and let it bubble slowly, 10 minutes, or until totally evaporated. Repeat with another 1/2 cup stock. Stir in the last 1/2 cup stock along with the milk. Adjust heat so the liquid bubbles very slowly. Partially cover the pot, and cook 1 hour. Stir frequently to check for sticking. Add the tomatoes, crushing them as they go into the pot. Cook, uncovered, at a very slow bubble another 45 minutes, or until the sauce resembles a thick, meaty stew. Season with salt and pepper.

Ricotta Torte

- 8 large eggs
- 1 tbsp vanilla
- 2 tsp grated orange zest

- 1 ½ cups sugar
- ½ cup all-purpose flour
- 6 cups whole-milk ricotta

Preheat oven to 350°F. Butter and flour a 9-inch spring form pan. Place the pan on a 12-inch square of heavy-duty aluminum foil, and mold the foil tightly around the pan so water cannot enter.

In a large bowl, beat the eggs, vanilla, and orange zest just until blended. Beat in the sugar and flour. In a food processor or blender, purée the ricotta until very smooth. Add the cheese to the egg mixture and stir well. Pour the batter into the prepared pan. Place the pan inside a large roasting pan and set it on the middle rack of the oven. Pour hot water to a depth of 1 inch into the roasting pan. Bake for 1 ½ hours, or until the top is golden and a knife inserted 2 inches from the center of the cake comes out clean.

Turn off the oven and prop the door open slightly. Let the cake cool for 30 minutes inside the oven. Remove from the oven and remove the foil wrapping. Cool completely on a wire rack.

The cake is best at room temperature or slightly chilled. Store in the refrigerator. Serves 12 to 16

Spanish Tapas Class, 2/28/07

- Tiny Meatballs in Saffron Sauce
- Bacalao with Garlic and Sherry
- Chorizo-filled Dates in Bacon
- Banderillas
- Marinated Asparagus Wrapped in Ham
- Spanish Potato Omelet
- Shrimp in Garlic Sauce
- Skewered Mushrooms and Bacon with Aioli
- Pa amb Tomàquet

We are indebted to Penelope Casas' wonderful books for many of these recipes.

Tiny Meatballs in Saffron Sauce

- ½ pound ground veal
- ½ pound ground pork
- 2 slices bacon, ground or very finely chopped
- 3 cloves garlic, minced
- 3 tbsp minced parsley
- 3 tbsp minced lettuce
- 1 egg, lightly beaten
- 1 slice bread, crusts removed, soaked in milk and squeezed dry
- 1 tsp coarse salt
- freshly ground pepper
- flour for dusting
- 2 tbsp olive oil
- 3 tbsp minced onions
- 1 tsp flour
- ¼ tsp smoked paprika
- ½ cup veal broth
- 2 tbsp white wine
- several strands saffron
- minced parsley for garnish

In a bowl mix together lightly the veal, pork, and bacon, half of the garlic, 1 tbsp of the parsley, the lettuce, egg, bread, salt, and pepper. Form into very small balls, not larger than 1 inch. Dust with flour.

Heat the oil in a shallow casserole large enough for all the meatballs. Brown the meatballs well on all sides. Add the onion and sauté until it is wilted. Sprinkle in the tsp of flour and the paprika and cook for a minute. Stir in the broth and wine, bring to a boil, cover, and simmer for 40 minutes.

Meanwhile, mash together in a mortar the remaining minced garlic, the remaining tbsp of parsley, the saffron, and a little salt. Stir this mixture into the meatballs, sprinkle with parsley, and serve.

These meatballs can be made several hours or a day in advance and reheated, but it is preferable to add the saffron mixture just before serving.

Bacalao (Salt Cod) with Garlic and Sherry

- 2 pounds skinned and boned dried salt cod,
- 5 tbsp olive oil
- 8 cloves garlic, minced
- 3 tsp paprika, preferably Spanish style
- ¾ cup dry (fino) Spanish sherry
- 4 tbsp minced parsley
- salt to taste

Soak the cod for 24-36 hours in cold water to cover at room temperature, changing the water occasionally. Drain and dry the cod well, then divide into tapas-size portions.

Heat the oil in a large skillet and sauté the cod until lightly golden on both sides. Transfer to a metal baking dish in which the cod fits snugly. To the oil in the skillet add half the minced garlic, the paprika, and the sherry. Boil for a minute, then pour over the cod. Sprinkle with the remaining minced garlic and parsley, and the salt. Bake at 350°F for 10-15 minutes.

Chorizo-Filled Dates in Bacon

- 1 chorizo sausage
- 12 pitted dried dates
- 3 slices bacon, cut in quarters crosswise
- oil for frying
- flour for dusting
- 1 egg, lightly beaten with 1 tsp water

Cut off the ends of the chorizo and slice the sausage crosswise into 3 equal pieces, about ¾ inch each in length (remove the skin if tough). Cut each of these pieces in half lengthwise and in half again, to make a total of 12 "sticks." (If your chorizo is thick, these pieces may be too large for the dates, in which case cut in half again.)

Insert each chorizo piece into a date and close the date around it. Wrap a strip of bacon around each date. Secure, if necessary, with a toothpick. Place the wrapped dates in a skillet with the seam side of the bacon down and sauté until the bacon is golden. Turn and brown on the other side. Drain on paper towels. You may now serve the dates or proceed to coat and fry them. If you are continuing, this step may also be done in advance.

Wipe out the skillet, then heat the oil at least ½ inch deep to about 380 °. Dust the dates with flour, and then dip them into the egg and immediately the hot oil. Fry until golden, turning once. Or, better, use a deep-fryer. Drain and serve.

Banderillas

Banderillas (the reference is from bull-fighting terminology) are tapas on a "dart" or toothpick with a flag, sort of like a cold mini shish kabob. The variations are almost endless.

- 1 small mushroom, stem removed
- 1 rolled anchovy, with or without caper
- a dab of mayonnaise
- 1 very small potato (or equivalent piece of a larger potato), boiled, peeled, and trimmed on the bottom to sit flat

- 1 rolled anchovy, with a caper
- 1 pitted cured black olive
- a dab of mayonnaise
- ½ small hard-boiled egg, cut crosswise, trimmed on the bottom to sit flat

- 1 cooked shrimp, shelled
- 1 cooked asparagus tip, about 2 inches long
- a dab of mayonnaise
- ½ small hard-boiled egg, cut crosswise, trimmed on the bottom to sit flat

Banderilla Dressing

This picada, a finely chopped mixture of parsley, garlic, pickle and oil, can be dabbed on any of the banderillas and gives an interesting added zest. Penelope Casas writes that this recipe comes from Tito of Madrid's *Bar Cascabel*, which specializes only in banderillas.

- 3 tbsp finely minced parsley
- 3 cloves garlic, finely minced
- 3 tbsp dill pickles or cornichons, finely minced
- 3 tbsp olive oil

Place the minced parsley, garlic, and pickle in the bowl of a processor or blender. With the motor running, add the oil gradually. Blend until as smooth as possible.

Marinated Asparagus Wrapped in Ham

- ½ pound thin asparagus, ends snapped off
- chicken broth
- salt
- 2 oz ham, thinly sliced, in 1 x 3-inch strips

Place asparagus in a skillet with a mixture of water and chicken broth just barely to cover. Bring to a boil, cover, and simmer for about 3-4 minutes- the asparagus should be tender but still crisp. Make sure you don't overcook them. Plunge into cold water to stop further cooking. Drain well and arrange in a single layer in a shallow bowl. Sprinkle with salt.

- ½ tsp Spanish paprika
- 3 tbsp olive oil
- 1 tbsp red wine vinegar
- salt and pepper
- ¼ tsp thyme
- 2 cloves garlic, sliced
- 2 tsp minced parsley
- 1 bay leaf
- 1 tbsp slivered onion

Whisk in the oil, vinegar, salt, pepper, paprika and thyme. Stir in the garlic, parsley, bay leaf, and onion. Mix well and pour over the asparagus.

Marinate, refrigerated, for several hours (but not overnight.) Remove the asparagus from the marinade and wrap a strip of the ham close to the stem end.

Spanish Potato Omelet, *Tortilla Española*

This classic is one of our all-time favorites.

- 1 cup olive oil
- 4 large potatoes, peeled and cut in 1/8" slices

- 1 large onion, thinly sliced
- coarse salt
- 4 large eggs

Heat oil in a medium skillet and add potato slices one at a time so they don't stick together. Alternate layers of potato with the onion slices and salt the layers lightly. Cook slowly over medium heat, lifting and turning the potatoes occasionally, until they are tender but not brown. Drain the potatoes in a colander, reserving about 4 tbsp of the oil.

Meanwhile, in a large bowl beat the eggs with a fork until they are slightly foamy. Salt the potatoes to taste and add to the beaten egg, pressing the potatoes down with a pancake turner so that they are completely covered. Let the mixture stand for 15 minutes.

Heat 2 tbsp of the reserved oil in the skillet until it reaches the smoking point (it must be very hot or the eggs will stick.) Add the potato and egg mixture, spreading it out rapidly in the skillet. Lower heat to medium-high and shake the pan often to prevent sticking. When the eggs begin to brown underneath, invert a plate of the same size over the skillet and flip the omelet onto the plate. Add the other 2 tbsp oil to the pan, then slide the omelet back into the skillet to brown on the other side. Lower the heat to medium and flip the omelet two or three more times to give it a good shape while it continues to cook. It should be juicy within. Transfer to a platter and cool, then cut in thin wedges or into 1-2" squares that can be picked up with toothpicks.

Shrimp in Garlic Sauce

- 2 lb shrimp, preferably very small, shelled
- coarse salt
- 8 tbsp olive oil
- 4 cloves garlic, very coarsely chopped
- 1 dried red chili pepper, stem and seeds removed, cut in 2 pieces
- ½ tsp Spanish paprika
- 2 tbsp minced parsley

Dry the shrimp well and sprinkle salt on both sides. Let sit at room temperature for 10 minutes. Heat the oil in four ramekins or one shallow 8-inch casserole. Add the garlic and chili pepper, and when the garlic just starts to turn golden (be careful not to overcook) add the shrimp.

Cook over medium-high heat, stirring, for about 2 minutes, or until the shrimp are just done. Sprinkle in the paprika, parsley, and salt. Serve immediately, right in the cooking dish if possible.

Skewered Bacon & Mushrooms

To make the Aioli:
- 1 cup mayonnaise
- 4 cloves garlic, mashed

- 1 tbsp olive oil
- 12 cubes about ½" each of slab bacon
- 12 medium mushroom caps

Make the sauce by combining the mayonnaise and garlic paste and letting stand at room temperature. Heat oil in skillet until very hot. Add bacon and mushrooms and stir-fry briefly until mushrooms are softened and bacon a little crisp. Spear bacon on a mushroom cap (right side up) and either dab with the aioli or pass it separately.

Catalan Garlic and Tomato Bread, *Pa amb Tomàquet*

- bread slices or rounds
- extra-virgin olive oil
- salt and pepper

- 1 very ripe tomato
- 4 garlic cloves, mashed

This typical Catalan tapa is very simple: bread — optionally toasted — with garlic and tomato rubbed over and seasoned with olive oil and salt. In many Catalan restaurants, the tomato mixture is pre-made and is brushed on the bread. If the mixture is not pre-made, there is said to be an ideal order to yield the best flavor. First, the garlic is rubbed on the bread. Then the tomato. Next the olive oil and finally salt to taste.

Oriental Dinner, 3/24/07

- **Eggplant with Walnuts and Garlic**
- **Baked Kibbeh with Topping**
- **Jeweled Rice**
- **Briwat, Rolled Baklawa**

There are countless versions of kibbeh, from a raw meat paste to little, oval shells stuffed with ground meat filling and drop-fried or cooked in yoghurt or bitter orange juice, as well as vegetarian kibbeh with pumpkin or potato, and one with fish-each version having a number of regional variations. One thing they all have in common is cracked bulgar wheat (*burghul* in Arabic).

Claudia Roden's unorthodox version of baked kibbeh is really delicious and very easy to make, it has only one layer of kibbeh and not two, with lots of the onion and pine nut filling as a topping instead. It can be served hot or cold as a main dish or cut up in small pieces as a *meza dish*.

See Briwat recipe, page 127.

Eggplant Slices with Walnuts and Garlic

This strongly flavored version of a very common meza dish originates in Georgia. The eggplant slices can be deep-fried or roasted in the oven as here. They should be served cold, and they can be made in advance.

- 2 pounds eggplant
- extra virgin olive oil
- 3 tbsp wine vinegar
- salt

- 6 garlic cloves, crushed
- 1/2 cup walnuts
- chopped flat-leaf parsley

Cut the eggplants lengthwise into slices about a quarter of an inch thick. Place on an oven tray and brush them generously with olive oil on both sides. Cook in an oven preheated to 475°F for about 20 minutes, or until lightly browned and soft, turning them over once.

Arrange them on flat serving plates, then brush with vinegar and sprinkle lightly with salt. Soften the garlic in 1 tbsp of olive oil over medium heat until the aroma rises, but do not let it color. Finely chop the walnuts in a food processor and mix with the chopped parsley in a bowl. Add the garlic with another tbsp of olive oil and sprinkling of salt, mix well, and spread this paste on the eggplant slices.

Serves 8 as an appetizer.

Baked Kibbeh with Onion and Pine Nut Topping

For Base:
- 2/3 cup fine-ground bulgar
- 1 onion, cut in quarters
- 1 pound lean lamb
- salt and black pepper
- 1 tsp cinnamon
- 2 tbsp vegetable oil

For Topping:
- 1 pound onions, sliced
- 3 tbsp extra virgin olive oil
- 1/3 cup pine nuts
- salt and black pepper
- ½ tsp ground cinnamon
- pinch of ground allspice
- 1 tbsp pomegranate molasses

For the base, rinse the bulgar in a fine sieve under cold running water and drain well. Purée the onion in the food processor. Add the meat, salt, pepper, and cinnamon and blend to a paste. Add the bulgur and blend to a smooth, soft paste.

With your hand, press the paste into the bottom of an oiled, rectangular baking dish. Flatten and smooth the top and rub with 2 tablespoons oil. With a pointed knife, cut the contents into 6 or 8 pieces. Bake in an oven preheated to 375°F for about 30 minutes, until browned.

While the base is baking, prepare the topping. Fry the sliced onions in the olive oil until they are golden brown, stirring often. Add the pine nuts and stir until lightly colored. Add a little salt and pepper, cinnamon, and allspice and the pomegranate molasses. Cook, stirring for a minute or so.

Serve the *kibbeh* with the topping spread over the top.

Peppery Bulgar Salad, *Kisir*

- 1 cup fine bulgar
- ½ cup boiling water
- 1 tbsp tomato paste
- juice of 1 ½ lemons
- 5 tbsp extra virgin olive oil
- ½ fresh chili pepper, finely chopped
- salt to taste
- 6 scallions
- 3 tomatoes, diced
- ¼ cup chopped parsley
- 2 tbsp chopped mint leaves
- 2 little gem or baby romaine lettuces

Put the bulgar into a bowl, pour the boiling water over it, stir, and leave for 15-20 minutes, until the grain is tender.

Add the tomato paste, lemon juice, olive oil and chili pepper, and mix thoroughly. Trim the green tops off the scallions, then slice them finely. Add them and the diced tomatoes to the bulgar mixture, together with the parsley and mint and mix well. Add salt to taste.

Serve with the small lettuce leaves stuck around the edges of the salad. Another way is to roll the bulgar mixture into oval balls the size of a small egg and to place each one in the hollow of the lettuce leaf.

Jeweled Rice with Dried Fruits

This is one of the glories of Persian cuisine and a favorite at wedding banquets, where it is meant to bring good luck and sweetness to the happy couple. Despite its sumptuous, exotic appearance, it is not that difficult to make.

- 3 cups white basmati rice
- 3 tbsp salt
- ½ cup dried apricots, quartered
- ½ cup golden raisins
- ½ cup dried cherries
- 8 tbsp unsalted butter
- ½ tsp ground cardamom
- ½ tsp freshly ground black pepper
- ½ cup coarsely chopped pistachios

Wash rice in several changes of cold water in a large bowl until water is almost clear. Let drain in a large sieve for several minutes. Bring 4 quarts water and salt to a boil in a 6-quart heavy pot. Add rice and boil, uncovered, stirring occasionally. Once the rice has absorbed all the liquid, but is still tender, remove the rice to a bowl.

Layer dried fruits and rice alternately in pot, beginning and ending with rice and mounding it loosely. Make 5 or 6 holes in rice to bottom of pot with handle of a wooden spoon. Cover pot with a kitchen towel and a heavy lid and fold edges of towel up over lid, so the towel won't burn. Cook over moderately low heat until rice is tender and crust has formed on bottom, 30 to 35 minutes. Remove from heat and let stand, tightly covered for at least 30 minutes.

Melt remaining 2 tbsp butter in a small skillet let over moderate heat. Add pistachios and cook, stirring, until toasted, about 2 minutes. Remove from heat. Spoon loose rice onto a platter. Dip bottom of pot in a large bowl of cold water for 30 seconds to loosen the crust. Remove crust with a large spoon and serve over rice. Sprinkle with pistachios.

Serves 8.

Two Paellas, 11/14/07

- **Potato Salad, *Ensaladilla***
- **Classic Paella**
- **Baked Tomato Paella**
- **Easy Flan**

Classic Paella

- 6 cups chicken broth
- 12 chicken thighs
- ½ lb chorizo, in ¼" slices
- ¼ lb Serrano ham, diced
- 1 lb medium shrimp, shelled
- 8 jumbo shrimp, with shells
- 3 cups paella rice
- ½ cup dry white wine
- 18 clams and/or mussels
- ½ tsp saffron
- 1 onion, peeled
- coarse salt
- ¼ tsp pimentón (smoked paprika)
- ½ cup olive oil
- 1 onion, chopped
- 8 scallions chopped
- 4 tbsp chopped garlic
- 2 roasted piquillo peppers
- 6 tbsp chopped parsley
- 2 bay leaves, crumbled.
- 1 cup fresh or frozen peas
- lemon wedges and parsley for garnish

Heat the broth with the saffron, pimentón and the whole onion. Cover and simmer 15 minutes. Remove the onion and measure the broth – you need exactly 5 ½ cups. Dry the chicken pieces well and sprinkle with salt. Heat oil in a 15" paella pan and fry chicken pieces over high heat until golden. Remove to a warm platter. Add the chorizo and ham to the pan and stir fry about 10 minutes. Add the chopped onion, scallions, garlic, and pimientos and sauté until the onion is wilted. Add the shrimp and sauté about 3 minutes more, or until the shrimp barely turn pink. Remove the shrimp to the platter with the chicken. Add the rice to the pan and stir to coat it well with the oil. Sprinkle in the chopped parsley and the crumbled bay leaves.

Stir in the wine, rice, and peas and then the chicken broth boiling hot. Salt to taste. Bring to a boil and cook, uncovered and stirring occasionally, over medium-high heat about 10 minutes. Bury the shrimp and the chicken in the rice. Add the clams and the mussels, pushing them into the rice, with the edge that will open facing up. Decorate the paella with the large shrimp, and cook on stovetop on low heat or bake at 325° F, uncovered, for 20 minutes. Before serving, let sit on top of the stove, lightly covered with foil for about 10 minutes.

Oven-baked Tomato Paella

- 3½ cups stock
- 1 medium onion, minced
- 1 tbsp minced garlic
- large pinch saffron threads
- 2 tsp Spanish pimentón (smoked paprika)
- 2 cups short-grain rice
- 1½ pounds ripe tomatoes, cored and cut into thick wedges
- salt and black pepper
- 1/4 cup extra virgin olive oil
- 1 tbsp tomato paste
- minced parsley for garnish

Preheat oven to 450°F. Warm stock in a saucepan. Put tomatoes in a medium bowl, sprinkle with salt and pepper drizzle with 2 tbsp olive oil. Toss to coat.

Put remaining oil in a 10- or 12-inch ovenproof skillet over medium-high heat. Add onion and garlic, sprinkle with salt and pepper, and cook, stirring occasionally, until vegetables soften, 3 to 5 minutes. Stir in tomato paste, saffron and paprika and cook for a minute or two more. Add rice and cook, stirring occasionally, until it is shiny, another minute or two. Add liquid and stir until just combined.

Put tomato wedges on top of rice and drizzle with juices that accumulated in bottom of bowl. Put pan in oven and bake. After 15 minutes, check to see if rice is dry and just tender. If not, return pan to oven for another 5 minutes. If rice looks too dry but still is not quite done, add a small amount of stock. When rice is ready, turn off oven and let pan sit for 10 minutes.

Remove pan from oven and sprinkle with parsley. If you like, put pan over high heat for a few minutes to develop a bit of a bottom crust before serving.

Serves 6-8.

Potato Salad, *Ensaladilla*

- 6 new potatoes
- 3 tbsp extra virgin olive oil
- 2 tbsp sherry wine vinegar
- ½ cup roasted piquillo peppers
- ½ medium onion, chopped
- ¼ cup capers
- ¼ cup fresh parsley
- 1 tbsp fresh chives
- 1 tbsp fresh basil
- 2 tsp fresh oregano
- ½ cup mayonnaise

Cut the potatoes in 1" cubes, and boil in salted water for 6 minutes. Drain and while still hot add the sherry wine vinegar. Stir lightly so that the potatoes absorb the vinegar. Add olive oil and stir again to coat the potatoes.

Add peppers, onions, capers, parsley, chives, basil, and oregano. Gently mix and place in refrigerator to cool. When ready to serve, add the mayonnaise and salt to taste.

Serves 6 as an appetizer.

Easy Flan

This is our eldest son Sebastian's other favorite dessert (after the Flourless Chocolate cake.)

- 1 ½ cups sugar
- 6 large eggs
- a 14oz can sweetened condensed milk
- two 13 oz cans evaporated milk
- 1 tsp vanilla

Preheat oven to 325°F. You will need 6 ramekins and a large baking pan to put them in.

Pour 1 cup sugar in warm pan over medium heat. Constantly stir sugar until it becomes caramel. Quickly pour about 2-3 tbsp of caramel in each ramekin, tilting it to swirl the caramel around the sides. Reheat caramel if it starts to harden.

In a mixer, blend the eggs together. Add in the milks first and then slowly mix in the remaining ½ cup of sugar, and then the vanilla. Blend smooth after each ingredient is added.

Pour custard into caramel lined ramekins. Place ramekins in a large glass or ceramic baking dish and fill with about 2 inches of hot water. Bake for 45 minutes in the water bath and check with a knife just to the side of the center. When knife comes out clean, the flans are ready.

Remove and let cool then place in refrigerator for at least an hour.

Invert each ramekin onto a small plate to serve.

Southern Italian Dinner, 3/7/09

- **Blood Orange Salad**
- **Sicilian Eggplant Relish**
- **Veal Saltimbocca**
- **Capellini d'Angeli Agli'e Olio**
- **Classic Cannoli**

This class has a Sicilian focus, and is also typical of the sunny shores of southern Italy. Blood oranges are a wonderful delicacy, deep-red in color, and bitter and sweet at the same time. They are usually available from December through April, and serve as the basis for a refreshing mid-winter salad.

Sicilian Eggplant Relish, *Capunatina*

- 2/3 cup olive oil
- 1 medium eggplant, peeled and diced
- salt and black pepper
- 1 cup onions, diced small
- 1 cup celery, diced small
- 2 cups fresh tomatoes, peeled, seeded and diced
- 12 Kalamata and 12 Sicilian olives, halved
- ¼ cup white raisins, soaked in water for 20 minutes, drained
- 1 tbsp capers
- 2 tbsp red wine vinegar
- 3 tbsp toasted pine nuts

In a large sauté pan, over medium heat, add ¼ cup of olive oil. When oil is hot, add eggplant. Season with salt and pepper. Sauté until eggplant is soft, about 15 minutes, stirring occasionally. Remove eggplant and set aside.

In the same pan, over medium heat, add 2 more tbsp of oil, and the onions. Season with salt and pepper. Sauté until wilted and lightly golden, about 4 minutes. Remove onions and set aside. Add 2 more tbsp of oil and cook celery. Season with salt and pepper. Sauté until wilted, about 3 minutes. Remove from pan and set aside.

Add the remaining oil. When oil is hot, add eggplant, onions, celery, tomatoes, olives, raisins, capers, vinegar, and pine nuts. Season with salt and pepper. Cook for about 15 minutes. Remove from heat and turn into a serving bowl. Let cool slightly and serve with crusty bread.

Serves 4-6 as an appetizer.

Blood Orange and Red Onion Salad

- 4 blood oranges
- 1 peeled small red onion
- salt and black pepper
- 4 tbsp extra-virgin olive oil

Peel blood oranges, removing pith with a paring knife. Cut oranges into 1/4"-thick slices and arrange on a serving platter. Thinly slice small red onion, and then scatter over orange slices. Season with salt and freshly cracked black pepper and drizzle with extra-virgin olive oil.

Serves 4-6.

Angel Hair Pasta with Garlic and Olive Oil, *Capellini d'Angelo Agli'e Olio*

- 8 garlic cloves, peeled
- 3 tsp chopped fresh parsley
- salt and pepper to taste
- fine bread crumbs
- ½ cup olive oil
- 1 lb cooked angel hair pasta

In a skillet, sauté garlic, parsley, salt, and pepper in oil over medium heat. When garlic just begins to turn brown, remove from heat. Toss entire contents with 1 lb cooked pasta. Serve with a sprinkle of toasted bread crumbs.

Veal Cutlets with Prosciutto and Sage,
Vitello Saltimbocca

- 8 thin veal cutlets (1/8" thick; about 3 oz each)
- 8 garlic cloves
- ½ tsp salt
- 24 fresh sage leaves
- 16 thin slices prosciutto
- flour for dredging
- ½ cup olive oil
- 2/3 cup dry white wine

Pat veal cutlets dry. Mince and mash garlic with salt to a paste. Spread about ½ tsp garlic paste on one side of a veal cutlet and arrange 3 sage leaves in one layer over paste. Cover veal cutlet with 2 slices prosciutto and secure prosciutto and sage with 3 wooden picks. Dredge in flour, then arrange veal cutlet, prosciutto side down, on a tray and season with pepper. Prepare the rest in the same manner.

In a large heavy skillet heat oil over high heat until it just begins to smoke and sauté 2 veal cutlets at a time, prosciutto sides down, 30 seconds. Turn veal cutlets over and sauté 15 seconds more, or until veal is just cooked through. Transfer veal with tongs to a platter and keep warm, loosely covered with foil. Sauté remaining veal cutlets and keep warm in same manner. Pour off oil from skillet and return skillet to high heat.

Add wine slowly and deglaze skillet, scraping up brown bits. Boil wine until reduced to about 1/3 cup. Discard wooden picks and serve saltimbocca drizzled with the sauce.

Serves 8.

Classic Cannoli

- 2 cups fresh ricotta
- 4 tbsp granulated sugar
- 1 tsp grated orange zest
- 1 tsp vanilla extract
- 10 pre-made cannoli shells
- powdered sugar for dusting

Beat together ricotta, sugar, orange zest and vanilla in a bowl with an electric mixer at medium speed 1 minute (do not overbeat). Cover and refrigerate until ready to use.

With the easy availability of excellent quality pre-made shells, there is no need to go into the effort to making your own shells.

Spoon filling into pastry bag and pipe some into 1 end of a cannoli shell, filling shell halfway, then pipe into other end. Repeat with remaining shells. Dust with powdered sugar. Makes 10.

Short Ribs for Roger, 2/7/09

- **Wilted Watercress Salad**
- **Classic Short Ribs with Egg Noodles**
- **Korean-style Beef Short Ribs**
- **Tiramisu**

Wilted Watercress Salad

- 2 bunches watercress
- 4 slices bacon
- ¼ cup apple cider vinegar
- 2 tbsp honey
- salt and pepper
- ½ tsp Dijon mustard

Rinse and clean watercress, removing the thick stems. Set aside. Heat a small non-stick pan on medium heat and cook the bacon until done, several minutes on each side. Remove the bacon from the pan and put on a paper towel.

Keep the bacon fat in the pan. Add cider vinegar and honey, and stir to dissolve. Sprinkle with salt and pepper, and add mustard. Taste and adjust seasoning. Bring the dressing to a simmer. Pour over the watercress. Crumble the bacon over the top. Toss and serve.

Serves 4 to 6 as a salad.

Korean Broiled Short Ribs, *Galbi*

- 2 lbs short ribs, boneless
- 5 tbsp sugar
- 3 tbsp oil
- 6 tbsp soy sauce

- 3 scallions, chopped
- 3 cloves garlic, minced
- dash of salt and pepper
- ¼ cup rice wine or sherry

Cut the ribs into 2" square pieces. Score both sides of each piece deeply with knife. Add sugar and oil to ribs. Mix well. Let stand.

Marinate 2 to 3 hours. Broil in a 475° F oven on both sides until well-browned. Combine remaining ingredients; mix well with ribs. Serve hot.

Serves 4-6 as an appetizer.

Classic Short Ribs

- 6 short ribs, trimmed, cut into 2" pieces
- kosher salt and ground black pepper
- 1/3 cup good olive oil
- 1 ½ cups chopped onion
- 5 stalks celery, diced
- 2 carrots, cut into 2" pieces
- 8 whole garlic cloves,
- 1 (750-ml) bottle dry red wine
- fresh thyme sprigs
- 6 cups beef stock
- 1 tbsp brown sugar
- 1 tbsp fennel seeds

Preheat oven to 400°F. Place the short ribs on a sheet pan, sprinkle with salt and pepper, and roast for 15 minutes or until brown. Remove from the oven. Reduce oven temperature to 300°F.

Meanwhile, heat the olive oil in a large Dutch oven and add the garlic, onion, celery, carrots, fennel seeds and cook over medium-low heat for 20 minutes, stirring occasionally. Pour the wine over the vegetables, bring to a boil, and cook over high heat until the liquid is reduced by half, about 10 minutes. Add about 1 tbsp salt and 1 tsp pepper. Add the thyme to the pot.

Place the roasted ribs on top of the vegetables and add the beef stock and brown sugar. Bring to a simmer over high heat. Cover and bake for 2 hours or until the meat is very tender.

Carefully remove the short ribs from the pot and set aside. Discard the herbs and skim the excess fat. Cook the vegetables and sauce over medium heat for 20 minutes, until reduced. Put the ribs back into the pot and heat through. Serve with the vegetables and the sauce over buttered egg noodles.

Serves 6.

Tiramisu

- 1 cup mascarpone
- 1 tsp lemon zest
- 2 tbsp sugar
- 2 tbsp Grand Marnier
- ½ cup chilled heavy cream

- 12 savoiardi (imported Italian ladyfingers)
- ½ cup brewed espresso at room temperature
- 4 oz semisweet chocolate, finely chopped

In a large bowl, whisk together the mascarpone, lemon zest and sugar until smooth. Pour the cream into the bowl of an electric mixer and whip the cream at high speed until it holds its shape softly when the beaters are lifted, about 4 minutes. Gently fold the cream into the mascarpone mixture.

Very lightly and quickly dip half of the savoiardi in the coffee. (Do not saturate them or they will fall apart.) Arrange the cookies in a single layer in a square or round serving dish, as you prefer. Spoon half of the mascarpone cream over the savoiardi and sprinkle with half of the chopped chocolate.

Repeat with remaining ingredients to create a second layer. Cover with plastic wrap and refrigerate for at least 1 hour, or overnight.

Serves 10-12.

A Persian-Turkish Feast, 2/16/09

- **Turkish Zucchini Fritters**
- **Turkish Beet Salad**
- **Persian Rice with Lamb, Apricots and Pistachios**
- **Persian Halva**

Turkish Zucchini Fritters

- 1 lb zucchini , grated
- 1 onion, coarsely chopped
- 3 tbsp vegetable oil
- 3 large eggs
- 3 tbsp all-purpose flour
- black pepper
- 6 sprigs of mint, fresh, chopped
- 3 sprigs fresh dill, chopped
- 8 oz feta cheese, mashed

Fry the onion in the oil over medium heat until soft and very lightly browned. Add grated zucchini and sauté, stirring, until soft.

Beat the eggs with the flour until well-blended. Add pepper and herbs and mix well. Fold in the feta cheese and then the onions and the zucchini.

Film the bottom of a non-stick pan with oil and fry a few at a time about 2 tbsp each, turning over once, until both sides are brown. Drain on paper towels and serve hot or cold. Serves 4

Beets with Yoghurt

- 1 lb small beets
- 2 tbsp lemon juice
- 2 tbsp olive oil
- 1 cup plain Greek yoghurt
- salt
- 1 tbsp finely chopped mint

Cut tops of beets off and roast until tender (about 1 hour.) Let cool for a few minutes, then peel and slice. Mix oil and lemon juice. Add yoghurt and salt and beat well, then mix with the beets. Pour into a serving dish and garnish with mint.

Serves 4

Persian Rice with Lamb, Apricots and Pistachios

- 2 cups basmati rice
- 6 tbsp melted butter
- 1 onion, finely chopped
- 1 pound lean lamb, cut into small cubes
- salt and pepper

- ½ tsp ground cinnamon
- ½ tsp allspice
- 1 cup tart dried apricots, cut in half
- 3 tbsp golden raisins
- 1/3 cup shelled unsalted pistachios

Wash the rice in warm water and rinse in a colander under cold water. Heat 2 tbsp of the butter in a pan and fry the onion until golden. Add the meat and sauté gently, turning the pieces to brown them all over. Add salt and pepper, cinnamon, allspice, and half of the apricots and raisins. Cover with water and simmer, covered, over low heat for 1-1½ hours, until the meat is very tender and has absorbed the sweet-and-acid flavors of the fruit.

Add water as required. After about an hour of cooking, add in the rest of the apricots

Boil the rice in a large heavy-bottomed pan for about 10 minutes. It will be a little underdone. Drain, and mix with 2 tbsp butter. Put the remaining butter in the bottom of the pan and mix in a ladle of rice.

Arrange alternate layers of rice and meat with the apricot sauce, starting and ending with a layer of rice. Cover and steam gently over very low heat for 20-30 minutes, until the rice is tender. A cloth stretched under the lid will absorb the steam and make the rice fluffier. Sprinkle with pistachios and serve, scraping up the crunchy rice from the bottom of the pan.

Serves 6.

Persian Halva

Also known as *halawa*, this is a very popular sweet found throughout the Middle East. Many are made with tahini or semolina flour. This Persian version uses a simple mixture of flour, sugar and butter with the sweet perfume of rosewater.

- 1 cup sugar
- ½ cup water
- ¼ cup rose water
- 4 threads saffron
- 8 oz unsalted butter
- 1 ½ cups flour
- shelled, hulled pistachios for garnish

Bring sugar and water to a boil in a saucepan over medium heat. Stir until all sugar is dissolved, and then add the rosewater and saffron. Cover, remove from heat and set aside.

Heat the butter in a large saucepan over low flame. Add the flour and stir to form a smooth paste. Continue to cook, stirring continuously, until the paste takes on a golden color, about 5-10 minutes.

Using a whisk, slowly beat the sugar syrup into the flour paste. Remove from heat and spread the halva paste evenly onto a plate or platter. Make attractive patterns on top of the paste using the back of a spoon or with a knife. Cover and chill until fully set. Decorate the top of the halva with whole pistachios. Cut into wedges and serve with tea or coffee.

Serves 6-8.

German Pork and Belgian Beer, 2/26/09

- **Braised Belgian Endive**
- **Fricadelles a la Bière**
- **German Parsleyed Potatoes**
- **Pork, Sausage and Beer-braised Sauerkraut**
- **Appelflappen**

Featuring Cooperstown's own
Ommegang Beers

Braised Belgian Endive

- 8 heads of Belgian Endive
- 2 tbsp butter
- 3 tbsp lemon juice
- ½ tsp salt
- 1 tbsp sugar

Halve, core and lightly sauté the endives in butter in a shallow pan. Turn after 1-2 minutes to sauté both sides. Add the remaining ingredients. Cover the pan and let simmer for about 10 minutes.

Serves 8.

German Parsleyed Potatoes, *Petersilienkartoffeln*

- 6 medium red potatoes
- 1 tbsp butter
- plenty of chopped parsley
- salt to taste

Peel potatoes and boil in salt water. Drain. Melt butter, add parsley, then potatoes and steam a few minutes.

Serves 4.

Belgian Meatballs in Beer Sauce, *Fricadelles á la Bière*

- 1 thick slice white bread, crusts removed
- 3 tbsp milk
- 1 lb ground beef
- ½ lb ground pork
- 1 egg
- salt
- black pepper
- ½ tsp nutmeg
- 2 tbsp flour
- 5 tbsp soft butter

Soak the bread in the milk and then knead into the meat together with the egg, salt, pepper and nutmeg. Form into 8 balls, dust in flour and sauté in 3 tbsp butter until golden brown. Make sure butter does not burn. Remove meatballs to platter.

- 1 medium onion, diced
- 1 tsp sugar
- salt to taste
- black pepper to taste
- 2 tbsp flour
- 1 cup beef broth
- 1 cup beer, **Ommegang Three Philosophers**
- 2 tbsp minced parsley for garnish

Discard all but 2 tbsp fat in the pan. Add the onion and sauté over low heat for about 10 minutes. Add the sugar, salt pepper and flour to the onions. Stir and cook another 1-2 minutes. Add the stock and beer and scrape all the brown bits up from the bottom of the pan. Reduce heat, return meatballs to the pan, cover and simmer until the meat is cooked through, about 45 minutes. Sprinkle with parsley and serve. Serves 4 (8 as an appetizer.)

Pork, Sausage and Beer-braised Sauerkraut

- 2 lbs sauerkraut
- 4 tbsp unsalted butter or duck, chicken, or goose fat
- ¼ lb apple-cured bacon, cut into ½" thick slices
- 3 onions, peeled and sliced
- 8 sprigs fresh thyme
- 2 bay leaves
- 2 tsp black peppercorns
- 12 juniper berries, lightly crushed
- 2 cups chicken stock
- 2 heads garlic, split in half crosswise
- 2 ham hocks, scored
- 2 cups **Ommegang Abbey Ale**
- 1 lb andouille sausage or kielbasa cut into 3" lengths
- 1 lb bratwurst cut into 3" lengths
- 4 thin boneless smoked pork chops
- mustard, for serving

Preheat oven to 325°F. Place the sauerkraut in a colander and rinse very briefly to remove some of the salt from the brine it is in. Press to release most of the excess liquid and set aside.

In a large non-reactive skillet, melt 3 tbsp of the butter over medium-low heat. Add bacon and cook until most of the fat is rendered, about 4 or 5 minutes. Add the onions and cook until they are soft but not browned. Transfer to a large Dutch oven. Add the drained sauerkraut and toss to combine.

Make a *bouquet garni* with thyme, bay leaves, peppercorns, juniper berries, and garlic. Add it in with the ham hocks, chicken stock and beer. Stir to combine. Cover and bake, until ham hocks are mostly tender, about 1 ½ hours. Meanwhile, melt the remaining tbsp of butter in a large skillet over high heat and brown the sausages and smoked pork chops on both sides. Set aside.

When the hocks are mostly tender, remove the casserole from the oven. Place the sausages on top of the sauerkraut. If the liquid has reduced to less than 2/3, add a bit more water. Cover and return it to the oven for about 30 minutes, or until the sausages are tender and heated through. Add the pork chops and press them into the sauerkraut. Cover and return to the oven and cook until pork chops are heated through and tender, about 30 minutes longer. Remove from the oven and discard the bouquet *garni*. Serve immediately, with each person receiving some of each of the sausages, part of a hock, part of a pork chop and some of the sauerkraut. Pass the mustard at the table.

Serves 8-10.

Dutch Apple Fritters, *Appelflappen*

- 2 ½ cups flour
- 1 ¼ cups beer, **Ommegang Witte Ale**
- ½ tsp salt

- 6 tart apples, peeled cored, and sliced ½" thick
- oil for deep frying
- powdered sugar for dusting

Combine flour, beer and salt and beat until smooth. Coat apple slices, a few at a time with batter and deep fry in the hot oil until light brown, about 3 to 4 minutes. Drain on paper towels and sprinkle with powdered sugar. Serve hot.

Makes about 30 fritters.

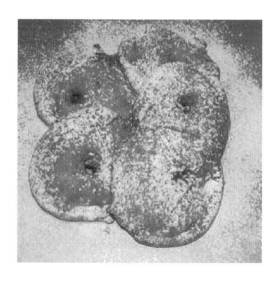

More Tapas for Dinner, 3/22/09

- Stir-fried Mushrooms, Shrimp, Ham and Peppers
- *Patatas Aioli*, Garlic Potatoes
- White Bean Salad
- *Lomo de Orza*, Marinated Pork Loin
- Chorizo in Red Wine
- Garlic-Lemon Chicken Strips
- Roasted Asparagus with Serrano Ham and Aioli
- Flourless Almond Cake

Stir-fried Mushrooms, Shrimp, Ham and Peppers

- 3 tbsp olive oil
- ½ green pepper, cut in ½-inch-wide strips
- ½ lb medium shrimp, shelled
- ½ lb mushrooms, in 1/4-inch-thick lengthwise slices
- 4 cloves garlic, minced
- ¼ lb cured ham, in ½ inch cubes
- 1/8 tsp crushed red pepper
- salt and black pepper
- 3 tbsp dry Spanish sherry
- 3 tbsp chicken broth

Heat 2 tbsp of the oil in a large non-stick pan. Stir-fry the green pepper over medium-high heat for a minute, then add the shrimp and stir-fry a minute more. Add mushrooms, garlic, ham, crushed red pepper, salt, pepper, and remaining tbsp of oil. Cook, stirring, until the mushrooms are softened. Add the sherry and broth, stir to deglaze the pan, and serve right away.

Serves 4 as an appetizer.

Patatas Aioli, Garlic Potatoes

- 4 lb red potatoes
- kosher or sea salt
- ½ cup of mayonnaise
- 3 cloves garlic, mashed to a paste
- 3 tbsp minced parsley

Bring potatoes to a boil in salted water, cover, and simmer for 15 minutes. Turn off heat and leave potatoes in the water, covered, until the potatoes are tender, about 15 minutes. Peel and cut the potatoes into 3/4 " chunks. In a bowl combine the mayonnaise, garlic, and parsley. The mayonnaise should be a little thin to combine smoothly with the potatoes - dilute with a little vinegar or fresh lemon juice if necessary. Fold potatoes in gently, season with salt and let sit for about 20 minutes at room temperature before serving. Or make ahead and refrigerate, then return to room temperature.

Serves 4.

White Bean Salad

- 1 lb or 1 can of white beans
- 1 red onion
- 1 green pepper
- 1 very ripe tomato
- 1 medium cucumber
- 1/4 cup black olives, chopped
- 4 tbsp extra-virgin olive oil
- 1 tbsp sherry vinegar
- 1 tsp salt

Rinse and drain the beans and place in a bowl. Cut vegetables into small pieces of equal size. Add olives. Prepare vinaigrette to taste and add to the mixture of vegetables and beans, taste for salt. Chill for 2 hours before serving. Serves 6.

Marinated Pork Loin, *Lomo de Orza*

- 1 lb boneless pork tenderloin, preferably with fat
- 1 cup extra virgin olive oil
- juice of half a lemon
- 3 cloves garlic
- 8 sprigs fresh thyme
- 8 sprigs fresh rosemary
- salt and black pepper

Cut pork loin into thick slices and then cut each slice in half lengthwise, place onto a plate and season both sides with salt and pepper. Heat some oil in a frying pan and cook pork over high heat for a few minutes on each side to color. When pork is a nice golden color, reduce heat to low and cook for a further 10-15 minutes until cooked through but still moist.

Meanwhile prepare the marinade. Finely chop the rosemary and thyme and place in bowl with lemon juice and olive oil. Peel and crush the garlic and add to the bowl. Mix well and season with salt and pepper. Once the pork is cooked through, transfer to a large *cazuela* or earthenware dish big enough so the pork covers the bottom in one layer. Pour marinade and any juices from the pan and add more olive oil if necessary to completely cover. Cover with foil and refrigerate overnight to marinate. Serve the next day with a generous drizzle of the marinade.

Serves 8 as an appetizer.

Chorizo in Red Wine

This dish is best prepared the day before you are planning to serve it.

- 1 large chorizo sausage
- ¾ cup Spanish red wine
- 2 tbsp brandy

- fresh flat leaf parsley, for garnish
- crusty bread, to serve

With a fork, prick the chorizo sausage in 4 or 5 places. Put it in a large pan and pour in the wine. Bring the wine to a boil, then reduce the heat and simmer gently, covered for 15-20 minutes. Transfer the chorizo and wine to a bowl or dish, then cover and let marinate for 8 hours or overnight.

The next day, remove the chorizo and reserve the wine for later. Carefully remove the outer casing from the chorizo and cut it into ¼-inch slices. Place the slices in a large, heavy-bottom skillet or flameproof serving dish over medium-high heat.

Pour the brandy into a small pan and heat gently. Now pour the brandy over the chorizo slices in the hot skillet, then stand well back and set alight. When the flames have died down, shake the pan gently, then add the reserved wine to the pan and cook over high heat until almost all of the wine has evaporated.

Serve piping hot, in the dish in which it was cooked, with parsley to garnish. Accompany with chunks or slices of bread to mop up the juices and provide toothpicks to spear the pieces of chorizo.

Serves 4-6 as an appetizer.

Garlic-Lemon Chicken Strips

- 4 large skinless, boneless chicken breasts
- 5 tbsp olive oil
- 1 onion, finely chopped
- 8 garlic cloves, finely chopped
- grated rind of 1 lemon, finely pared rind of 1 lemon and juice of both lemons
- 4 tbsp chopped parsley, plus extra to garnish
- salt and pepper
- lemon wedges and crusty bread to serve

Using a sharp knife, slice the chicken breasts widthwise into very thin slices. Heat the olive oil in a large, heavy-bottom skillet, then add the onion and cook for 5 minutes, or until softened but not browned. Add the garlic and cook for an additional 30 seconds.

Add the sliced chicken to the skillet and cook gently for 5-10 minutes, stirring from time to time, until all the ingredients are lightly browned and chicken is tender. Add the grated lemon rind and lemon juice and let it bubble. At the same time, deglaze the skillet by scraping and stirring all the bits on the bottom of the skillet into the juices with a wooden spoon.

Remove skillet from the heat, then stir in parsley and season to taste with salt and pepper. Transfer, piping hot, to a warmed serving dish. Sprinkle with the pared lemon rind and garnish with the parsley. Serve with lemon wedges for squeezing over the chicken, accompanied by chunks or slices of crusty bread for mopping up the lemon and garlic juices.

Serves 6-8 as an appetizer.

Roasted Asparagus wrapped in Ham

- 3 tbsp olive oil
- 6 slices Serrano ham or prosciutto, each cut in 1/2 lengthwise

- 12 asparagus spears, trimmed
- black pepper

Preheat oven to 400°F. Grease a cookie sheet with some of the olive oil. Wrap a piece of ham around the asparagus, and place on the cookie sheet. Brush the ham and asparagus with the remaining olive oil, and season with pepper. Roast for 10 minutes (depending on the thickness of the asparagus) until tender, but still firm.

Serve with Aioli, below.

Makes 12.

Aioli

- 2/3 cup mayonnaise
- 2 tbsp fresh lemon juice
- 2 cloves garlic, minced

- ¼ tsp salt
- ¼ tsp freshly ground black pepper

Mix ingredients together in a food processor until well blended.

Flourless Almond Cake

- 9 oz almond flour
- thinly pared strip each of lemon and orange zest
- 2 tbsp of butter
- 1 tbsp flour
- 6 eggs
- 9 oz extra fine sugar

Preheat oven to 450°F.

Grease a shallow spring-release or plain cake pan with butter and dust it with flour. Blanch the zest, place in a food processor with almond flour and combine. Separate the yolks from the whites. Beat together the yolks, sugar and ground almonds in a food processor.

Whisk the egg whites to dry peaks, fold them into the cake mixture and pour into the prepared pan. Put into the oven, turn heat down to 300° F and bake for half an hour or until a fine skewer stuck into the center of cake comes out clean.

Normandy Dinner Class, 3/13/09

- Green Salad with Apples and Camembert Toasts
- Moules Marinières
- Galettes Bretons
- Pork Loin with Apples and Calvados
- Gâteau Breton

Green Salad with Apple Dressing and Camembert Toasts

- 3 tbsp apple cider vinegar
- salt and pepper
- 3 tbsp walnut oil
- 1 large apple, cored, cut into 1/2-inch pieces
- 8 oz Camembert cheese
- 16 thin diagonal baguette slices, lightly toasted
- 8 cups mixed salad greens

Whisk vinegar and oil in large bowl to blend. Season to taste with salt and pepper. Stir in apple pieces. Let apple marinate at room temperature about 30 minutes, stirring occasionally.

Spread Camembert evenly over toasts, dividing equally. Add greens to apple dressing; toss to coat. Season with salt and pepper. Divide among plates and serve each with 2 cheese toasts.

Serves 8.

Moules Marinières

- 4 tbsp unsalted butter
- 6 tbsp chopped shallots
- 2 tbsp minced garlic
- 4 sprigs parsley
- 4 sprigs thyme
- 4 sprigs tarragon
- 4 lbs mussels (about 4 dozen), well scrubbed, rinsed, and de-bearded
- 1 cup dry white wine
- salt and pepper
- 3 tbsp chopped parsley leaves

In a large deep sauté pan or pot, melt butter over medium-high heat. Add shallots, garlic, and herb sprigs, and cook, stirring, until fragrant and the shallots are soft, about 1 minute.

Add wine, pepper, and salt and bring to a boil. Add the mussels, cover and cook, shaking the pan occasionally, until the mussels are opened, 5 to 6 minutes.

Remove from the heat and discard any mussels that have not opened. Transfer the mussels and their liquid to a large, deep serving bowl and garnish with the chopped parsley. Serve immediately.

Serves 4 as a main course, 8 as an appetizer.

French Bread Croutons

- 1 (12 to 15-inch) loaf French or Italian bread, cut into ¼ to ½ -inch slices
- 2 cloves garlic, peeled and sliced in half
- 1/4 cup olive oil
- 1/4 tsp salt
- 1/8 tsp freshly ground pepper

Preheat oven to 400ºF. Place bread slices on a large baking sheet and brush 1 side of each slice first with the cut garlic cloves and then with the olive oil, and then lightly season with the salt and pepper. Bake until light golden brown, about 8 minutes. Cool slightly on the baking sheet before handling or serving.   Makes about 16 croutons.

Pork Loin with Apples, Hard Cider and Calvados

- 5 lb pork loin roast, trimmed
- 1 tbsp flour
- salt and black pepper
- 2 tsp finely chopped rosemary
- 4 tbsp butter
- 3 medium onions, diced
- 6 cloves garlic, chopped
- 4 stalks rosemary
- 5 baking apples, cored and quartered
- 1/2 cup hard cider
- 1/4 cup calvados

Preheat oven to 325°F. Tie the pork loin every 2" with twine so that it holds a round shape. In a small bowl, mix flour, salt and pepper to taste, and chopped rosemary. Rub the flour mixture all over the pork loin, coating well.

Heat 2 tbsp butter in a large heavy skillet and sear meat over high heat, until browned on all sides. Transfer with pan juices to a large baking pan. Scatter onions and garlic around the roast. Cut up remaining butter and distribute evenly atop onions. Add rosemary stalks. Cover with foil and place in oven. Cook for 45 minutes, and then add apples and hard cider. Baste with pan juices. Re-cover and cook 30 minutes more. Raise oven temperature to 400°F, remove foil, baste, and cook for another 15 minutes.

Place roast on a cutting board, remove string, and allow to rest for 10 minutes before slicing. Meanwhile, transfer onions and apples to a platter. On top of the stove, reduce pan juices by half. Warm the calvados in a little pot, add to the pan juices, and flame. Simmer the sauce while you slice the pork loin. Arrange meat over apples and onions and serve with the sauce.

Serves 8-10.

Buckwheat Crepes, *Galettes Breton*

- 1 cup buckwheat flour
- 1 cup all-purpose flour
- 4 large eggs
- 1 cup milk
- ½ tsp sea salt
- 4 tbsp butter, melted butter for the pan
- ¾ cup water

Blend flour, eggs, milk, salt and melted butter with the water at high speed until smooth, about 2 minutes, scraping down the sides. Strain the batter through a fine-mesh sieve. Cover and let rest, refrigerated, for at least an hour or overnight. The batter may thicken once it has rested and may need to be thinned with water. Heat a nonstick pan over medium heat until a sprinkle of water sizzles in it. With a paper towel, spread butter over the pan, being sure to wipe most of it off. Pour enough batter to just cover the pan then swirl the batter around until it covers the whole surface. Adjust the heat to medium-low. When the edges of the galette begin to turn golden and move away from the pan, about 3 minutes, lift the edge nearest to you using a spatula. Flip over and cook the second side just long enough for it to set, less than a minute. Remove from the pan and start a stack, using wax paper to layer.

Shrimp Filling

- 1 lb medium shrimp, shelled, de-veined, tails removed and cut into chunks
- 1 tbsp butter
- ½ cup dry white wine
- ½ cup heavy cream
- ¼ tsp sea salt
- 1/8 tsp black pepper
- 1 tbsp chopped tarragon
- juice of half a lemon
- ¼ cup crème fraîche
- 2 leeks, cleaned, trimmed and chopped

In a large sauté pan, melt the butter and sauté the leeks over low heat until tender, about 5 minutes. Add wine, cream, salt and pepper and simmer gently until reduced by two-thirds. Add shrimp and stir until pink, about 5 minutes. Stir the tarragon, lemon juice and crème fraîche into the mixture. Spoon about one-half cup of the mixture onto a buckwheat crepe, fold in half and serve immediately.

Gâteau Breton

- 1 ½ cups cake flour
- ¾ cup sugar
- 6 large egg yolks
- 1 cup unsalted butter, cut in cubes
- 10" spring form pan

Preheat the oven to 375°F. Butter the pan thoroughly on all sides. Take 1 tsp of the egg yolks, add 1 tbsp water, and mix to create the glaze. Set aside.

Put flour in a bowl, stir in sugar, add the butter and egg yolks. With paddle attachment of a mixer, slowly mix until dough is smooth and golden. Scoop dough into the pan, and smooth the top.

Brush cake with glaze, and mark a lattice design on top with the tines of a fork (in a diamond type pattern.) Bake 15 minutes, turn oven down to 350°F and bake 25 minutes more until it is golden on top and firm to the touch.

Let cake cool completely in the pan before unmolding.

Serves 8-10.

Fresh, Local and Organic, 3/27/09

- **Shiitake and Chevre Tart**
- **Roasted Lamb Chops with Chermoula and Asparagus**
- **Walnut Maple Torte with Maple Meringue Frosting**

Shiitake and Chèvre Tart

- 1 ½ cups all purpose flour
- ¼ tsp salt

- ¾ cup (1½ sticks) chilled unsalted butter
- ¼ cup ice water

Blend flour and salt in a food processor. Add butter and process until a coarse meal forms. Add ice water; process until moist clumps form. Gather dough into ball; flatten into disk. Wrap in plastic and chill 30 minutes (or up to a day before.)

Soften slightly before rolling out. Preheat oven to 375°F. Roll out dough on floured surface to 15-inch round. Transfer to 9-inch-diameter tart pan with removable bottom, and trim off excess dough. Freeze crust 20 minutes. Line crust with foil. Fill with dried beans or pie weights. Bake until sides are set, about 20 minutes. Remove foil and beans; bake until pale golden, piercing with toothpick if crust bubbles, about 15 minutes. Cool. Maintain oven temperature.

- 1 ½ cups whipping cream
- 6 garlic cloves, peeled
- 1 large egg
- ¼ tsp salt
- 1 tbsp olive oil

- 8 oz fresh shiitake mushrooms, stemmed, sliced
- 4 oz goat cheese at room temperature

Bring cream and garlic to boil in heavy medium saucepan. Reduce heat to medium; simmer until mixture is reduced to 1 cup, whisking occasionally, about 15 minutes. Cool. Puree in processor. Blend in egg and salt.

In the meantime, heat oil in a large skillet over medium-high heat. Add mushrooms and sauté until tender, about 5 minutes. Season with salt and pepper. Cool. Spread goat cheese over bottom of crust. Sprinkle mushrooms over. Spoon cream mixture over. Bake until filling is set, about 20 minutes. Cool on rack.

Serves 6.

Roasted Lamb Chops with Chermoula and Asparagus

Chermoula is a marinade used in Algerian, Moroccan and Tunisian cooking usually used on seafood, but can be used on meats or vegetables.

- 1 tbsp cumin seeds
- 1 ½ cups parsley
- ½ cup fresh mint leaves
- ½ cup fresh cilantro
- 3 garlic cloves
- 1 tbsp sweet paprika
- 1 tsp coarse kosher salt
- ¼ tsp cayenne pepper
- 6 tbsp extra-virgin olive oil, divided
- 1 tbsp fresh lemon juice

Heat a small skillet over medium heat. Add cumin seeds and toast until aromatic and slightly darker, stirring occasionally, about 2 minutes. Transfer to processor. Add herbs, garlic and seasonings. Using on/off turns, pulse until a coarse paste forms, then gradually add 4 tbsp of the oil. Transfer 2 tbsp chermoula to small bowl; whisk in lemon juice and remaining 2 tbsp oil. Cover and chill to serve with lamb.

- 8 lamb loin chops
- 1 tbsp butter
- 1 tbsp extra-virgin olive oil
- 4 tbsp chopped shallots
- 1 ½ pounds asparagus, trimmed, cut into 3" pieces
- salt and pepper
- 2 tsp finely grated lemon peel

Transfer remaining chermoula to large re-sealable plastic bag. Add lamb chops; seal bag and turn to coat well. Chill at least 4 and up to 24 hours. Put lamb and chermoula in a Ziploc bag and let stand at room temperature 1 hour. Preheat oven to 500°F. Line rimmed baking sheet with foil. Place rack on prepared baking sheet. Place lamb on rack and sprinkle with salt and pepper. Roast until 130°F (for medium-rare) about 13 minutes. Transfer to platter and let rest 5 minutes.

Melt butter with 1 tbsp oil in large heavy skillet over high heat. Add asparagus and sauté until tender, stirring often, about 3 minutes. Add shallot and lemon peel. Sauté 1 minute. Place 2 lamb chops and divide the asparagus on each plate. Drizzle with chermoula.

Serves 4.

Walnut Maple Torte

- 1 cup walnuts
- 1 cup cake flour
- 1 ½ tsp baking powder
- 2 tsp espresso powder
- 1 tbsp boiling-hot water
- 1 ½ sticks unsalted butter
- ¾ cup sugar
- 3 large eggs
- 2 tbsp vegetable oil
- 6 ounces cream cheese, softened
- 6 tbsp pure maple syrup

Preheat oven to 350°F. Butter and flour two 8-inch round cake pans, knocking out excess flour. On a baking sheet toast walnuts in middle of oven until 1 shade darker, about 8 minutes. Cool, then grind walnuts fine in a processor. Sift together flour, baking powder, and a pinch of salt. In a small cup stir together espresso powder and water. In a large bowl with an electric mixer beat together butter and sugar until light and fluffy and add the eggs one at a time, beating well after each addition. Beat in flour mixture, espresso, walnuts and oil until just combined.

Spoon batter into cake pans, smoothing tops, and bake in middle of oven about 25 minutes, or until pale golden and a tester comes out clean. Cool cake layers in pans on a rack 15 minutes. Run a thin knife around edges of pans and invert cake layers onto rack to cool completely. In a small bowl beat together cream cheese and 2 tbsp maple syrup until smooth. Place first layer on an ovenproof serving plate and with a pastry brush gently brush top with 1 ½ tbsp maple syrup. Spread cream cheese mixture evenly onto layer and top with second layer. Brush top of torte with remaining 1 ½ tbsp maple syrup.

Maple Meringue Frosting

- 2 large egg whites
- 1 cup pure maple syrup

- ¼ tsp cream of tartar

Let whites stand at room temperature 1 hour. In a 1-quart heavy saucepan bring maple syrup to a boil over moderate heat and simmer until a candy thermometer registers 235° F. (be careful it doesn't bubble over).

While maple syrup is simmering, in bowl of a standing electric mixer beat whites with cream of tartar and a pinch of salt until they just hold stiff peaks. Add hot maple syrup in a stream, beating until meringue is thickened and glossy, 1 to 2 minutes. Preheat broiler.

Immediately frost torte with a narrow metal spatula, mounding extra meringue on top and drawing it up with a fork to form peaks. Broil torte about 4 inches from heat until tops of peaks are pale golden, about 30 seconds. Let torte stand at room temperature 15 minutes before serving.

Northern Italian Dinner, 11/7/08

- Priest's Soup, *Minestra del Prete*
- Appetizers, *Antipasti*
- Braised Pork Ribs with Polenta
- Tiramisu (see recipe page 171.)

Priest's Soup, *Minestra del Prete*

- 5 tbsp unsalted butter
- 4 large eggs
- 4 oz mortadella
- 2 cups freshly-grated parmesan
- 3 tbsp semolina flour
- salt, black pepper
- 8 cups good chicken stock

Preheat oven to 375°F. Grease an 8" square cake pan with 1 tbsp butter. In a bowl, whisk the eggs into a froth. Beat in 1 ½ cups parmesan cheese, 4 tbsp melted butter and the ground mortadella. Finally, fold in 3 tbsp semolina flour. Bake 10-15 minutes. Remove, cool and let sit overnight. Cut into ½ inch dice, and spread out on a platter to dry.

To make the soup, bring the stock to a lively bubble in a 4 quart saucepan. Season with salt and pepper. Add the croutons and then pour the soup into a tureen or ladle it into soup dishes. Pass the remaining parmesan separately.

Serves 6-8 as a first course.

Braised Pork Ribs with Polenta

- 5 lbs lean country-style pork spare-ribs
- 1 large onion, minced
- 2 large bay leaves
- ground cloves, allspice and cinnamon to taste
- 1 cup dry red wine
- ½ cup small black olives, pitted
- 4 tbsp extra-virgin olive oil
- 5 tbsp minced parsley
- 2 large cloves garlic
- ¼ tsp black pepper
- two 16 oz cans plum tomatoes with their liquid
- 4 tbsp chopped fresh basil
- salt and pepper to taste

Note that the meat can be cooked 1 day ahead. Cover and refrigerate overnight. Gently reheat before serving. A little water or broth may be needed to moisten the meat. Trim excess fat from the meat. If it is in one piece, separate into pieces by cutting between the ribs. Heat the oil in a 12" sauté pan over medium-high heat. Add the meat in single layers. Take about 20 minutes to brown slowly, until dark brown and crusty on all sides. Set aside on a platter.

Keep the heat at medium, and stir in the onion and parsley. Cook 10 minutes or until golden-brown, taking care not to burn the brown glaze in the bottom of the pan. Stir frequently. Stir in the garlic, bay leaves and generous pinch each of the spices. Return meat to the pan, turning to coat with the vegetables and seasonings. Pour in the wine, adjusting the heat so that it bubbles slowly. As the wine cooks down (10-15 minutes) use a spatula to scrape up the brown bits on the bottom of the pan. Break up the tomatoes as you them to the pan. Stir in the olives and bring mixture to a very slow bubble over low heat. Now cover tightly and cook over low heat about an hour.

Add the basil, cover and cook at a gentle bubble another 30 minutes or until the meat is tender. Season with salt and pepper. Skim any fat from surface, then spoon over hot polenta and serve.

Serves 8-10.

Creamy Quick Polenta

- 4 cups water
- 1 cup medium-grain yellow corn meal
- salt to taste
- 4 tablespoons butter
- 1 cup cream cheese

Heat lightly salted water to a boil over high heat, about 5 minutes. Quickly whisk in the polenta until fully incorporated. Lower the heat to a low simmer, add the butter and allow the polenta to cook, stirring occasionally, for 30 minutes. Finish by stirring in the cream cheese and salt to taste. Stir vigorously to fluff. Serves 8.

Vegetables dipped in Olive Oil, *Pinzimonio*

- 1 fennel bulb
- 1 bunch celery
- 2 carrots
- 1 heirloom tomato
- 1 radicchio
- 1 bell pepper
- extra-virgin olive oil
- salt and pepper to taste

One of the best-known Tuscan antipasti. *Pinzimonio* relies on the freshest vegetables and your best olive oil. Simply clean and slice vegetables, and arrange on a platter with a small bowl of olive oil to which you have added salt and freshly ground pepper.

Bocconcini di Prosciutto

- 4 oz   gorgonzola
- 1 oz   heavy cream
- 18 walnuts halved
- 18 prunes, pitted
- 18 thin slices prosciutto or speck

Mix the cheese with the cream in a bowl insert some into prune. Cover with a walnut half. Wrap with prosciutto and hold together with a toothpick.

Makes 18.

Fall Harvest Dinner, 10/24/08

- *Torta Miranda*, Paduan-style
- Roasted Beet, Walnut and Gorgonzola Salad
- Harvest Stew Stuffed in Pumpkins
- Upside-down Pear Skillet Cake

Torta Miranda, Paduan-style

- 2 cups flour
- 1 tsp salt
- 8 tbsp chilled unsalted butter, in pieces
- 1 egg, lightly beaten
- 1 tbsp cream

To make the dough, which is a very short pastry, combine salt and flour in bowl. Mix the butter in food processor or with a pastry blender until the mixture resembles cornmeal. Make a well in the center and add the cream and egg. Mix together with a fork and gather the dough into a ball. Wrap well in plastic wrap and chill for at least 20 minutes. Makes two 9" crusts.

- 2 tbsp olive oil
- 2 onions, thinly sliced
- 2 lbs spinach or kale, washed and trimmed
- 1 lb smoked pork, diced
- a pinch each of allspice, salt and black pepper
- 1 lb ricotta cheese, drained
- 4 eggs, lightly beaten

Heat oil and add the onions. Cover and cook over very low heat for about 15 minutes. Cook spinach in a second, dry pan, until wilted, then drain and cool for a few minutes. Squeeze out excess water and chop coarsely. Combine with onions, pork, ricotta, allspice and eggs, and mix well. Add salt and pepper to taste.

Preheat oven to 425°F. Oil a 9" pie pan, and press half the dough into the bottom of it. Brush with oil, then add the filling, and cover with the other half of the pastry. Trim excess pastry and fold and pinch edges. Make a vent in the center, and bake about 40 minutes or until crust is golden. Cool and serve.

Serves 6-8.

Roasted Beet, Walnut and Gorgonzola Salad

- 12 small beets, cleaned and trimmed
- 6 tbsp fig-balsamic drizzle
- 2/3 cup chopped walnuts
- 12 tbsp extra-virgin olive oil
- 1 cup crumbled Gorgonzola cheese

Preheat oven to 400°F. Toss beets in 2 tbsp of the oil, then lay on baking sheet, and cover tightly with foil, enclosing completely. Bake until fork-tender. Toast the walnuts for about 5-8 minutes, or until they just start to brown. Let the beets cool, then peel and slice. Whisk the remaining olive oil and the balsamic drizzle in a bowl to blend thoroughly. Pour the dressing over the warm beets. Divide among the individual plates. Sprinkle with the cheese and toasted walnuts, and serve warm.

Harvest Stew Stuffed in Pumpkins or Squash

- coarse salt and freshly-ground black pepper
- 12 oz green beans, trimmed
- 6 small 1-2lb pumpkins or acorn or carnival squashes, seeded, top removed and reserved
- 12 chicken legs and thighs, skin-on
- 2 tbsp unsalted butter
- 8 oz whole peeled chestnuts
- 3 leeks, halved, dark green parts discarded, rinsed well and cut diagonally into 1 ½" slices
- 6 carrots, cut diagonally in 1" slices
- 18 Brussels sprouts, trimmed
- 1 cup olive oil
- 1 cup chicken stock
- 3 Honey Crisp apples, quartered
- 1 lb small potatoes, quartered
- 2 turnips, cut into eighths
- 4 cloves, thinly-sliced garlic
- 1 celery root, peeled and cut in 1" cubes
- 3/4 cup packed flat-leaf parsley, coarsely chopped

Prepare an ice-water bath in a large bowl. Bring a large pot of salted water to a boil. Add Brussels sprouts, and cook until just bright green an crisp-tender. With a slotted spoon, remove to ice water bath to stop cooking. Repeat with green beans. Drain and set vegetables aside.

Preheat oven to 375°F. Rub inside of pumpkins or squashes with oil, then place on a sheet in the oven. Roast until tender, but still holding its shape, about 30 minutes.

Heat 1 tbsp oil in a large skillet over medium-high heat. Season the chicken parts generously with salt and pepper. Working in batches of 2-3, cook chicken until golden-brown, about 3-4 minutes per side. Remove excess fat from skillet. Repeat with remaining chicken, each time adding 1 tbsp oil. Add the stock to the skillet, and bring to a boil, scraping bottom of skillet to deglaze. Pour into a small bowl to cool.

Place chicken on a baking sheet, and roast in the oven until golden-brown and cooked through, about 40 minutes. Reserve pan juices.

Combine potatoes, leeks, carrots, turnips, and celery root in a large bowl. Toss with remaining olive oil, and season with salt and pepper. Spread vegetables in a single layer on a rimmed baking sheet, and roast until golden-tender, about 40 minutes. Add the blanched sprouts and green beans, as well as the apples, chestnuts and garlic, and toss together. Roast until the garlic is golden-brown, and the vegetables thoroughly heated through or about 10 minutes.

Combine all the cooked ingredients with the stock and the reserved pan juices in a large bowl. Mix well, then place some in each pumpkin or squash. Roast about 5-8 minutes.

Fill each with vegetables and 2 pieces of chicken and serve.

Serves 6.

Vanessa's Upside-down Pear Skillet Cake

- 1 cup brown sugar
- 1 1/3 cup flour
- 2 tsp cinnamon
- ½ tsp salt
- 2 large eggs
- ½ cup vegetable oil

- 3 oz unsalted butter
- 1 1/3 cup sugar
- 1 ¼ tsp baking soda
- 2 small pears, grated
- 4-6 ripe pears, peeled, cored and sliced lengthwise

Preheat oven to 350°F. Put the brown sugar and the butter into a cast-iron skillet, and place in oven about 5 minutes or until brown sugar melts. Remove skillet from oven.

Arrange the pear slices in the bottom of the skillet, to cover.

Mix together eggs, oil, sugar and grated pear.

Mix dry ingredients together in a separate bowl, then add to the wet ingredients. Mix to form a batter, and pour over the pears.

Bake for about an hour, or until "springy" to the touch. Cool for 20 minutes, then invert and remove from skillet to a large serving plate.

*Photographs are courtesy Veronica Seaver, Vanessa Daou,
Antony Daou, Black Cat Ventures LLC or public domain.*

Sources and Bibliography

- Serena Bass, *Serena, Food and Stories*
- Mark Bittman, NYT, *The Minimalist,* various columns
- Bon Appétit, *various, 1987, 1998, 2003*
- Anna Teresa Callen, *The Wonderful World of Pizzas, Quiches and Savory Pies*
- Penelope Casas, *Food and Wine of Spain*
- Penelope Casas, *Tapas The Little Dishes of Spain*
- Julia Child and Jacques Pépin, *Julia and Jacques Cooking at Home*
- Craig Claiborne, *The New York Times Cookbook*
- Bernard Clayton, *Soups and Stews*
- Marion Cunningham, *The Breakfast Book*
- Marion Cunningham, *The Fannie Farmer Cookbook*
- Lorenza de'Medici, *Lorenza's Antipasti*
- Ina Garten, *Barefoot Contessa*
- Ina Garten, *Barefoot in Paris*
- The Gourmet Cookbook, 2004 edition
- Gourmet Magazine , *various 1985, 1994, 1997, 1998*
- Maida Heatter, *Maida Heatter's Book of Great American Desserts*
- Maida Heatter, *Maida Heatter's Book of Great Desserts*
- Maida Heatter, *Maida Heatter's Cakes*
- Anissa Helou , *Lebanese Cuisine*
- Madhur Jaffrey, *Climbing the Mango Trees*
- Mollie Katzen, *Moosewood Cookbook*
- Mollie Katzen, *The Enchanted Broccoli Forest*
- Emeril Lagasse, *Food Network*
- LaTienda.com
- Nigella Lawson, *How To Be A Domestic Goddess*
- Alice Medrich, *Cocolat*
- Frank Mentesana and Jerome Audereau, *Once Upon A Tart*
- Parragon Books, *Tapas*
- Jacques Pépin , *Fast Food My Way*
- Jacques Pépin, *Today's Gourmet*
- Claudia Roden, *Arabesque*
- Claudia Roden, *The New Book of Middle Eastern Food*

- Judy Rosenberg, *Rosie's Bakery All-Butter, Fresh Cream, Sugar-Packed, No-Holds-Barred Baking Book*
- Lynne Rossetto-Kasper, *The Splendid Table*
- Julee Rosso and Sheila Lukins, *The Silver Palate Cookbook*
- Round the World Cooking Library, *Dutch and Belgian Cooking*
- Habeeb Salloum, *The Toronto Star*, January 2009
- Suvir Saran, *American Masala*
- Saveur Magazine, various issues
- Michele Sciccolone, *La Dolce Vita*
- Nancy Silverton, *Pastries from La Brea Bakery*
- Martha Stewart Living magazine, *January 2009*
- Molly Stevens, *Bon Appétit, April 2007*
- Anna Thomas, *Vegetarian Epicure*
- David Waltuck and Melicia Phillips, *Staff Meals from Chanterelle*
- Patricia Wells, *At Home in Provence*
- Patricia Wells, *The Provence Cookbook*
- Patricia Wells, *Trattoria*
- Paula Wolfert, *Couscous and Other Good Food from Morocco*
- Paula Wolfert, *Mediterranean Cooking*
- Wikipedia, *various*

And of course, the Black Cat Café.

Black Cat

Made in the USA
Charleston, SC
15 July 2010